Living God's Word

Reflections on the Sunday Readings
for Year B

Archbishop Terrence Prendergast

NOVALIS

© 2011 Novalis Publishing Inc.

Cover design and layout: Audrey Wells

Cover art: "Evangelista Marco" - mosaico realizzato dalla Scuola Mosaicisti del Friuli (Spilimbergo PN - Italia), a.s. 1960/1961, bozzetto di Padre Leo Coppens [Mosaic created by The School of Mosaic of Friuli (Spilimbergo, PN - Italy), 1960/1961, sketch by Fr. Leo Coppens.]

Published by Novalis

Publishing Office
10 Lower Spadina Avenue, Suite 400
Toronto, Ontario, Canada
M5V 2Z2

Head Office
4475 Frontenac Street
Montréal, Québec, Canada
H2H 2S2

www.novalis.ca

ISBN: 978-2-89646-323-7

Cataloguing in Publication is available from Library and Archives Canada.

Printed in Canada.

We acknowledge the financial support of the Government of Canada through the Canada Book Fund for business development activities.

5   4   3   2   1   15   14   13   12   11

Dedication

SODALIBUS SOCIETATIS JESU

TO MY BROTHER JESUITS

"Whoever does the will of God is my brother
and sister and mother..."

(Mark 3.35)

Acknowledgements

Over a ten-year period, it was my privilege to write a weekly set of reflections on the Sunday readings ("God's Word on Sunday") in the Toronto-based *Catholic Register*.

On several occasions, friends and associates suggested that these be made available in book form as an aid to those who have the challenge of providing homiletical reflections for parish and other faith communities. As well, I have been told that liturgy committees and study groups that gather to pray over the Scriptures in preparation for their participation in the Sunday Eucharist appreciate these reflections.

Joseph Sinasac of Novalis, who was my editor at the *Register*, prodded me to select the best of my earlier work and to write new reflections to cover any gaps in the columns caused either by an early start to Lent or by the late resumption of continuous readings after Pentecost. I am grateful for his encouragement and patience.

My thanks go, too, to Anne Louise Mahoney, whose competent, efficient and speedy work in copy editing brought consistency, harmony and clarity to a text that had gestated over a number of years.

The present collection of readings is from the liturgical year of Mark (designated "Year B" in lectionaries), for which I have a predilection, as this gospel was the subject of my doctoral dissertation, *"Without Understanding" (Mark 7.18): A Redaction-Critical Study of the References to the Disciples' Lack of Understanding in Mark's Gospel* [Toronto: Regis College, 1977].

That study was an attempt to discover this theme of incomprehension by the disciples in the tradition before it came to Mark, and then to trace Mark's development of it as he, like a good preacher addressing a congregation each week, exposed it within his vision of the gospel message.

For Mark, the account of disciples struggling to grasp the gospel message and overcoming resistance to its implications for daily life is ultimately "good news". Indeed, the gospel signals humanity's incapacity to achieve salvation while simultaneously laying out God's gracious promise of new life for all who follow Jesus through death to new life.

Completing a thesis or a collection of essays on the weekly Sunday readings is not unlike the disciples' passage from darkness to light, from incomprehension or resistance to the Good News to understanding and acceptance of it.

As I commend this aid to Sunday worship to disciples aspiring to deepen their knowledge and love of the Scriptures, I am conscious of my own debt to teachers and ministers of the word who have assisted me: several Jesuit confreres have helped me immensely, as have scholar-friends in the Catholic Biblical Association of America, whose annual conventions were always a joy, and the scholarly communities where I spent refreshing sabbatical years – the Pontifical Biblical Institute in Rome (1987–88) and the École biblique in Jerusalem (1994–95).

May these associates rejoice in seeing handed on ideas and expressions I have gleaned from their academic labours. Any inadequacy in transmitting their research remains entirely my own responsibility.

This work is dedicated in homage to my brother Jesuits in the year and on the day when I observe the Golden Jubilee of my entry into the Society of Jesus.

The Company of Jesus has truly become my family in Christ. Their encouragement of my reading, praying, studying, preaching and teaching God's word – in tandem with the *Spiritual Exercises* of Holy Father Ignatius – is a gift I continue to cherish.

+Terrence Prendergast, S.J.
Archbishop of Ottawa
August 14, 2011

Contents

Foreword

When I began going through Archbishop Terrence Prendergast's reflections on the Sunday readings, *Living God's Word*, the memories of the 2008 Synod on the Word of God in the Life and Mission of the Church came flooding back. Both the Synod and the post-synodal apostolic exhortation by Pope Benedict XVI in 2010 call for deeper reflection on the Word of God, recognizing that it is God who speaks and that our response is one of faith rooted in the sacred Scriptures. In the exhortation, we are all reminded that the home of the Word of God is the Church and the liturgy is the privileged setting for that Word. The same document tells us of the importance of the homily, and the special bond between the lectionary and the homily. In *Living God's Word*, Archbishop Prendergast brings together all of these enriching ideas and helps to "break open" the Word of God precisely in the context of the Sunday liturgy.

On our own we would never understand who God is, the great gift of the Word made flesh and the enlivening power of the Holy Spirit. God's living Word is recorded in sacred Scripture and beautifully presented to us in the readings of the liturgy. But even here we need some help. In *Living God's Word*, Archbishop Prendergast walks us through the Sunday readings of Year B, helping the reader to grasp more fully the meaning of God's Word and to embrace it in the context of that privileged expression of Scripture – the liturgy.

Living God's Word is a thoughtful guide to texts as varied as they are profound. With a master teacher's skill, Archbishop Prendergast guides the reader through the Scriptures, offering helpful insights, explanations of the Greek or Hebrew words from which the English translations are derived, and details that enrich our appreciation for the times in which Jesus taught and how out of the ordinary his ministry was to his contemporaries.

In a particular way, Archbishop Prendergast highlights the "disciples' lack of understanding," which he notes is a major theme in Mark's Gospel. This incomprehension is not so different from what Christians face in our secular culture today, in which we are called to enter into the Church's New Evangelization. Somehow, in what we do and how we express our faith, we have to be able to repropose, present all over again, our belief in Christ and his Gospel to those who are convinced that they already know the faith and it holds no interest for them – those who lack understanding. We have to invite them to hear God's Word all over again, because perhaps the first time, the message simply was not heard. Like Mark and the first disciples, we are called by God to share his revelation with others so they might come to know who God is.

As we face the call for the renewal of culture today, we are reminded that we must first know deeply our faith and then be willing to share it. The prayerful reading of the Scriptures in communion with the Church, as presented in *Living God's Word*, is an effective way to deepen our understanding of Jesus and his mission, and at the same time grow in the confidence needed to share the message.

Our Holy Father, Pope Benedict XVI, in the 2008 Synod on the Word of God and in his apostolic exhortation *Verbum Domini* (2010), calls the Church to more frequent prayerful reading of the Scriptures. While the liturgy will always be a unique home for the proclamation of the Word of God, the Synod highlighted the blessings that come from opening the Bible in a wide range of other situations, so that the Word of God can nurture us in our homes, workplaces or wherever else we gather. Our Holy Father noted that "the Scripture is to be proclaimed, heard, read, received and experienced as the word of God, in the stream of the apostolic Tradition from which it is inseparable."

In this "stream of the apostolic Tradition," Archbishop Prendergast's reflections can help individuals, Bible study groups, catechists, parents and adult faith formation gatherings as they read the Sunday Scriptures to prepare their hearts before participating in Sunday's Mass. *Living God's Word* also is a helpful tool for priests and deacons in preparing their homilies. It is precisely at the liturgy, which is both an act of worship and a teacher of the faith, that the vast majority of practising Catholics come into contact with the Scriptures.

Every believer is obliged not only to hear the Word of God, but to share it. Christ is our teacher. He offers his people the words of truth and everlasting life. "For this I was born and for this I came into the world, to testify to the truth" (John 18.37). Today his teaching mission endures in those whom he sends.

Carrying out that challenge will be easier for all of us thanks to the work of Archbishop Prendergast.

His Eminence Donald Cardinal Wuerl
Archbishop of Washington

Introduction

I. The Year of Mark

In this volume, the background reflections for the Sunday scriptural readings are taken from the liturgical year designated by the letter "B", which features continuous readings from the Gospel of Mark.

Gospel passages on several Sundays after Christmas, during Lent, in Eastertide, as well as the 17th to 21st Sundays in Ordinary Time, are taken from the Gospel of John. Except for the mid-year readings of John, a similar process happens in Year "A", which is devoted to Matthew's Gospel, and in Year "C", when the selections are taken from the Gospel of Luke.

Reflections on the Solemnities of Our Lord, the Blessed Virgin Mary and other important feasts of saints, of all the faithful departed, and of the dedication of the Basilica Cathedral of St. John Lateran – which can displace the Sunday celebration in Ordinary Time – are found in *Living God's Word: Reflections on the Sunday Readings for Year A* (Novalis, 2010).

Generally speaking, the first reading, which is from the Old Testament (except in Eastertide, when selections from the Acts of the Apostles are featured), has been chosen to complement the gospel passage, either by anticipating the message of Jesus or some truth about him (sometimes related as biblical prophecy to its fulfillment in Christ), or otherwise presenting similar themes to those found in the gospel.

The second reading is generally from one of the letters of St. Paul or another apostolic author (James, Jude, Peter, John), and parts of it are usually read over a number of Sundays in a row (depending on the length of the letter).

Given the above configuration of scriptural readings, my weekly reflection usually centres on the gospel, with references of shorter or longer length on the first reading and, as space permits, a brief allusion to the second reading.

On occasion, because of the importance of the text or to offer a variety in the focus of the homily, my attention falls on the second reading or, less frequently still, on the psalm.

II. Introduction to the Gospel of Mark

Scholars remain divided about several aspects concerning this shortest of the gospels, which in recent decades has enjoyed new attention because it has been perceived as the earliest gospel brought to completion and, in many academic circles, one of the base texts for the Gospels of Matthew and Luke.

Many interpreters locate the composition of Mark just prior to, or shortly after, the fall of Jerusalem in 70 AD. Traditionally, the author has been associated with Peter's testimony, writing either for the Church in Rome or for some other community facing persecution.

Mark's story begins with John the Baptist

Mark describes the preaching of Jesus as issuing God's demand to the Galileans of his time to change their hearts because, through Jesus' preaching, God's kingdom had arrived in their midst ("The time is fulfilled, and the kingdom of God has come near; repent, and believe in the Good News" [1.15]).

The calling of disciples

Mark follows Jesus' call to conversion with peremptory commands to four individuals – Simon [Peter] and Andrew, James and John – to leave their occupation (fishing) and family (Zebedee) in order to fish with Jesus for people to inhabit God's kingdom.

Jesus' invitation for his disciples to have a change of outlook touches them negatively and positively. Negatively, discipleship meant leaving their way of life and former ties. Positively, it meant following Jesus. Henceforth, they would not only accompany Jesus, but he would let them share his ministry and eventually continue it.

As the gospel proceeds, we see these and other disciples called to "be with him and to be sent out to proclaim the message", even having authority to cast out demons as Jesus did (3.14-15). Jesus' disciples will be invited to an ongoing rethinking of their outlook on life – to conversion.

Summary statements

Well on into his narrative, Mark recounts crowd reactions to Jesus' presence: "Wherever he went, into villages or cities or farms, they laid the sick in the marketplaces, and begged him that they might touch even the fringe of his cloak; and all who touched it were healed" (6.56).

The perceptive reader notes that, in this summary statement, the evangelist has generalized the story of the woman who had been suffering from hemorrhages for twelve years (5.25-34).

The healing acts are complemented by a summary statement that generalizes both the exorcism and the cure: "The whole city was gathered around the door. And he cured many who were sick with various diseases, and cast out many demons ..." (1.33-34a).

Secrecy and discovery

Mark also profited from the occasion of his summary statement about multiple exorcisms to add an interpretive comment, "and he would not permit the demons to speak, because they knew him" (1.34b).

Mark took Jesus' command to silence – a traditional aspect of exorcism rituals – and gave it his own significance ("because they knew him"). Thus did Mark introduce a key motif of his gospel – the veiling of Jesus' identity. This theme, designated by some scholars as "Mark's messianic secret", is explored more fully in the account of Jesus cleansing a leper (1.40-45).

As we come to see, in Mark's Gospel perspective, the demons know who Jesus is, and his enemies quickly grasp who he claims to be, while the crowds wonder about him and the disciples seem

ARCHBISHOP TERRENCE PRENDERGAST

to be utterly lacking in understanding of the truths he strove to communicate.

The first manifestation of this sorry inner state of the disciples appears when Simon and his companions "hunted for" Jesus in the wilderness, where he had gone to pray early in the morning "while it was still very dark" (1.35). Their outlook must be deduced from their statement about the crowds that had gathered at the door of Simon Peter's house the night before ("Everyone is searching for you"). They imply that there are reasons – perhaps not selflessly motivated ones – for him to go back with them to the crowds.

Jesus revealed – we may surmise that this was the result of his early morning prayer – that he had other priorities and, in a typically hopeful outlook, included them in his company and plans ("Let us go on to the neighbouring towns, so that I may proclaim the message there also" [1.38; cf. 14.42a]). Marvellously, the disciples, though uncomprehending, are called to join Jesus in heralding the message of the kingdom and casting out demons.

What Jesus taught of God's kingdom – what was then beginning to hold sway over human lives – he would later enact in the miracle of the loaves.

In the structure of the lectionary, the selections in mid-summer leave Mark's account of the first miracle of the loaves in favour of the account found in the Fourth Gospel, along with the subsequent Johannine "Bread of Life" discourse (John 6.1-69); it is proclaimed on the 17th to 20th Sundays in Ordinary Time.

The disciples' lack of understanding

In the early Church, the disciples of Jesus struggled for several decades with the issue of whether and under what conditions Gentiles might become participants in God's covenant. Those Jews who had been and still considered themselves members of the faith community of Israel asked themselves whether the Gentiles who came to believe in Jesus had to become observers of the Jewish religious and dietary rules. In effect, the question was whether the Gentiles had to become Jews before becoming Christian.

As the conclusion to the controversy in Mark 7.1-15, Jesus articulated the startling truth that "there is nothing outside a person that by going in can defile, but the things that come out are what defile". Next, the disciples again "enter the house" (in Mark, the place where Jesus gave them private instruction) and asked Jesus to explain his puzzling statement (7.15-21).

First, Jesus expressed surprise that the disciples had not understood his parabolic saying ("do you also fail to understand?" [7.18; cf. 4.13]). We will see this motif recur as the gospel narrative develops and the disciples' incomprehension becomes a pervasive leitmotif.

Restoring hearing, speech, sight

In Jesus' healing of a deaf-mute (Mark 7.31-37), it has been noted that the original meaning of the Greek word for a hearing-impaired person means "blunt" or "dull". Several Old Testament texts associate deafness with the Gentiles because of their presumed insensitivity to God's word (cf. Isaiah 42.17-19; 43.8-9; Micah 7.16).

In a healing gesture, Jesus thrust his fingers into the man's ears, perhaps suggesting the creation of a passageway for the evil spirit, causing the deafness to depart. The act of spitting – probably on his fingertips – reflects the ancient belief that the saliva of powerful people had curative qualities. Since Jesus is someone saturated with the Spirit, his spittle, charged with holiness, is able to destroy demonic forces holding a person in bondage.

Still, because such gestures appeared magical, some rabbis opposed the use of spittle for therapeutic purposes. The fact that neither Matthew nor Luke transmits this tradition may indicate that some in the early Church shared such reservations about Jesus' actions in this healing.

A similar mix of a touching gesture and words may be seen in the equally difficult miracle of the restoration of sight to the blind man of Bethsaida (cf. Mark 8.22-26).

Spiritual deafness and blindness

Taken together, the parallel healings of someone struggling to hear and speak plainly with that of a blind man who comes to sight

ARCHBISHOP TERRENCE PRENDERGAST

in stages suggest what Jesus intends to do so that the Twelve and, indeed, each disciple might see, speak and hear spiritually ("Do you have eyes, and fail to see? Do you have ears, and fail to hear?" [8.18]).

We are told about the cure in graphic terms: "immediately [the man's] ears were opened, his tongue was released [from bondage to the evil spirit?], and he spoke plainly" (7.35). Then Jesus charged the people to tell no one about what had happened. As is often the case in Mark, however, there is no holding back proclamation of what Jesus is able to effect in healing people – signs of the arrival of God's kingdom.

Confession at Caesarea Philippi

The confession at Caesarea Philippi constitutes the centrepiece of Mark's Gospel. The whole first half of the gospel revealed universal wonderment about Jesus' identity (for example, "Who then is this, that even the wind and the sea obey him?" [4.4]). Until Peter's confession at Caesarea Philippi, the disciples were in a stupor, bewildered and confused. But a breakthrough occurs. On behalf of his fellow disciples, Peter confesses that Jesus is the Christ, God's anointed one, the Messiah.

From the encounter and confession at Caesarea Philippi onwards, Jesus and the disciples are on a journey. They are "on the way" (8.27; 9.33, 34; 10.17, 32, 46, 52), a phrase that gets charged with meaning because it stands for what it means to be a "follower" or "disciple" of Jesus. (The Greek text reads "on the way" in Mark 10.17, 32 and 46, even if these words are rendered variously in the English translation as "on the road", "on a journey", "came to".) During this phase we see a recurring pattern: 1) Jesus predicts his coming suffering and death; 2) the disciples say or do something to show that they don't understand or don't accept what he is saying; and 3) Jesus then patiently gives them new teaching to draw out the implications of his teaching about the paradoxical way of life he espouses.

Resistance to the Cross

During the journey south through Galilee to Capernaum, Jesus enunciated the second and least detailed of three passion predictions

(9.30-32; cf. 8.31-33 and 10.32-34). Jesus foretold that the Son of Man would be betrayed into human hands, with few details supplied. However, the passive verb form "will be betrayed" indicates that God is to be involved in what happens to Jesus, including the fact that three days after he has been put to death, he will rise again. The disciples' reaction is characterized by their fear – often associated with a lack of faith, in Mark's Gospel – and by their not understanding.

The theme of the disciples' lack of understanding is a major one in Mark (cf. Mark 4.13; 6.52; 7.18; 8.14-21); there are also hints of this same motif (e.g. 5.31; 6.37; 9.6). While at times this incomprehension has intellectual aspects, generally the disciples do grasp that, if Jesus were to fulfill the role of the Christ through the path of suffering, this would have implications for their lives as well.

It is this truth that the disciples rebel against (cf. Peter's reaction to the first passion prediction in 8.32-33) or oppose by acting in ways contrary to the teaching of Jesus. Here is the issue underlying their argument about which of them was the greatest. Their failure in understanding, then, is as much about behaviour as it is about intellectual perception.

Jesus' new teaching addresses the central issue by calling the Twelve to new behaviour patterns: anyone who wants to be first must become last of all and servant of all.

Identifying with the child

Jesus embodied this teaching by taking in his arms one who was last of all in the culture of his day – a child. Since modern times, our society has tended to romanticize children, stressing qualities such as their innocence, dependence, vulnerability and openness. Though the Greco-Roman culture at times idealized the child's innocence, a more prevalent outlook stressed the ideal of leaving childhood behind for the full humanity of adulthood. Similarly, in the biblical world, childhood was something to be left behind for maturity in God's sight.

Thus, Jesus, by identifying himself ("whoever welcomes one such child in my name welcomes me") and the Father who sent him ("whoever welcomes me welcomes not me but the one who sent me" [9.37]) with the inconsequential child, radically challenged the prevailing ideals of the Jewish and Hellenistic world views. He also laid out an upside-down image of what greatness means in God's kingdom.

This is the kind of earth-shaking teaching that remains as challenging to us in our day as it was to the disciples in theirs. Also, it is as radically new as the teaching of God's will manifest in the cross and resurrection of Jesus. In effect, the transforming power of Christ's cross and resurrection can be found in his teaching on service to all and on the way one receives little children.

The strange exorcist

In the gospel, Jesus invited his disciples to embrace a tolerant spirit when several of them tried to curtail an exorcist found casting out demons in his name. Speaking for the Twelve, John said that they had forbidden the exorcist "because he was not following us" (9.38).

In reply, Jesus admonished them, saying they should not put constraints on such an exorcist. For he argued that such a person could not simultaneously use Jesus' name to perform an exorcism and "soon afterward" speak evil of him. For "whoever is not against us is for us" (9.39).

Still, this same Jesus on another occasion uttered a saying that seems narrower and less open ("whoever is not with me is against me, and whoever does not gather with me scatters" [cf. Matthew 12.30]). And yet, despite appearances, these sayings of Jesus need not be contradictory, particularly if the former was spoken to the disciples about themselves and the latter to those indifferent about his message as far as it concerned them.

Hard sayings on scandal, divorce

Jesus' view on divorce is a widely attested aspect of his teaching found in the New Testament (cf. Matthew 5.32; 19.6, 9; Mark 10.9; Luke 16.18; 1 Corinthians 7.11). However, sorting out the nuances of his sayings on divorce is complex. Interpreters may overlook his teaching on marriage.

Jesus taught that God had created man and woman so that they might be joined together in the unity of one flesh in marriage.

The lectionary's introduction to the passage on marriage omits the setting given by Mark's narrative, namely that Jesus left Capernaum and went to the region of Judea and beyond the Jordan, where crowds gathered and Jesus taught them (10.1).

This passage, with the gospel message of Jesus, challenges the believer to have an ordered life. The things of God (wisdom, God's will) come first. With such an orientation to life, health, the length of one's life, the career one embraces and material goods can be rightly ordered. Without such ordering, no one can be saved!

The rich young man Jesus loved

Next, the gospel presents a budding Solomon seeking wisdom or meaning for his life. This man's search was urgent, for he ran up and knelt before Jesus, inquiring, "What must I do to inherit eternal life?"

While Jesus' reply may seem generic, listing commandments that deal with interpersonal relationships, closer examination shows it to be crafted to the man's circumstances, and specifically to his wealth. For, after listing the commandments against murder, adultery and stealing, Jesus substitutes the injunction "you shall not defraud" for the commandment against coveting. Perhaps Jesus is suggesting that those with riches do not need to covet (having everything already), but are consumed with increasing their wealth through fraud.

Heaving a sigh of relief, the man blurted out a marvellous confession of goodness, noting that he had guarded against all these things since his youth. Next comes the statement that Jesus looked intently at him and "loved him". Given that Jesus had recently placed his arms around a child (9.36) and the intensity of his gaze (which is lost in the lectionary's translation "looking at him"), we may imagine Jesus putting his arm around the man's shoulder before confiding to him that, in contrast with the commandments he had observed, "You lack one thing: Go, sell what you own, and give the money to the poor … then come, follow me" (10.21).

ARCHBISHOP TERRENCE PRENDERGAST

Jesus promised that upon selling his possessions, the man would have "treasure in heaven". This likely is equivalent to "inherit[ing] eternal life", which the man had asked about when he came to Jesus.

The man's heart was revealed to have been attached to his riches, rendering him unwilling or unable to follow through on his inquiry about what he had to do to inherit eternal life: "When [the man] heard this, he was shocked and went away grieving, for he had many possessions" (10.22).

Jesus drew for his startled disciples the corollary that those who have riches find it hard to enter God's kingdom because of their propensity to be attached to what they have rather than to God's will: "Children, how hard it is to enter the kingdom of God! It is easier for a camel to go through the eye of a needle than for someone who is rich to enter the kingdom of God" (10.25).

The explosiveness of Jesus' teaching is shown in the amazement of the disciples, which finds an echo in the hearts of disciples in every age, including our own.

The impossibility of entering the kingdom without God's help ("for God all things are possible") implies a demand to leave all things "for my sake and for the sake of the good news" and thereby gain the "hundredfold" of a new family among disciples "in this age ... and in the age to come, eternal life" (10.27, 30-31). In seeking God's will above all else, the disciple finds himself or herself to be blessed beyond measure.

In Mark 8.27–10.52, the evangelist depicted Jesus on a "journey" towards his passion, death and resurrection in Jerusalem. "On the way," he tells his disciples how his manner of life is to touch every aspect of their lives: marriage, divorce and the family (10.1-12), humility and service in the community (10.13-16, 35-45) and, lastly, one's attitude towards material possessions or riches.

In all of this divine catechesis, we find the disciples continually struggling with Jesus' teaching (indeed, often misunderstanding it). But we see as well his continual patience as he spells out for them the "way of the kingdom".

Finally, the closing words of that gospel pericope (passage) reassure us that God cannot be outdone in generosity: whatever we surrender for the kingdom will be made up for in new relationships and in a new freedom with regard to the blessings of this world and the world to come. "There is no one who will not receive a hundredfold ... now in this age ... and in the world to come, eternal life" (10.29-30).

Glory and authority among disciples

To the Twelve Jesus explained that in the kingdom of God, things had to be different than in a world of power relationships ("among the Gentiles those whom they recognize as their rulers lord it over them" [10.42]). Jesus' way is summarized in a couple of maxims: "Whoever wishes to become great among you must be your servant, and whoever wishes to be first among you must be slave of all" (10.43-44).

The example of Bartimaeus

Bartimaeus is the second blind man to whom Jesus brings healing in Mark's Gospel. The healing of the blind man of Bethsaida, a town in Galilee and the home of Simon and Andrew, took place in stages (cf. 8.22-26), as does the healing of the son of Timaeus. Each story also suggests implications for the faith life of a believing disciple.

After Jesus had put saliva on the eyes of the Bethsaida blind man and laid hands on him, he asked the man whether he could see anything. At first the man could see indistinctly ("I can see people, but they look like trees, walking" [8.24]). Then Jesus told him to look again "and he saw everything clearly" (8.25).

In a way, this act of "looking again" may be understood to characterize all Jesus' teaching about his forthcoming Passion (8.31–10.45). In this extended instructional unit, Jesus invited his disciples to see anew what it meant to be the followers of a crucified Messiah. For the cross contains stirring implications for one's outlook on lifetime goals (8.34–9.1), authority in the community (9.33-37), marriage, divorce and family (10.2-16), wealth and possessions (10.17-31), and leadership in the kingdom (10.35-45).

ARCHBISHOP TERRENCE PRENDERGAST

As Jesus went on teaching his disciples, they gradually moved towards Jerusalem in a weakened state of mind ("Jesus was walking ahead of them; they were amazed, and those who followed were afraid" [10.32]).

Finally, they come to Jericho, one of the oldest known human settlements and the entry point for the Israelites when they had come into the Promised Land. The City of Palms stands as a liminal place; Bartimaeus would prove a model disciple.

His acclamation "Jesus, Son of David, have mercy on me!" (10.47) anticipated the welcome Jesus would receive in Jerusalem as heir to David's throne. Though the blind man's voice was but one voice in the crowd, people were impatient to get to the Holy City, so they attempted to silence Bartimaeus ("many sternly ordered him to be quiet" [10.48]).

But above the hubbub, Jesus had heard his plea, stopped and invited him to draw near. Suddenly the crowd's reaction changed: "Take heart; get up, he is calling you" (10.49).

Bartimaeus spontaneously leapt up, abandoning his cloak and naming his deepest desire: "My teacher, let me see again" (10.51).

Once Jesus healed Bartimaeus, he did not "go" away – now healed by his faith – as Jesus had directed. Rather, after regaining his sight, he began to follow Jesus "on the way" (10.52: terminology that suggests more than the road – a call to Jerusalem, Calvary and the fulfillment of the Father's will).

Bartimaeus' response was the reverse of the rich man who would not follow Jesus; his enthusiasm was the opposite of the amazement, hesitation and fear of the Twelve and others on the journey with Jesus.

And Bartimaeus' healing epitomized what Jesus was about in teaching his disciples: namely, healing their spiritual blindness, something that would not be complete until after his death and resurrection.

The Passion Narrative

Three passion predictions had given the reader an outline of Jesus' sufferings: how he would be handed over to the chief priests and scribes, condemned to death, given over to the Gentiles, mocked, spat upon, flogged and killed, before rising from the dead after three days (cf. 10.32-34).

This schema is completed with other traditional elements of the Passion: Jesus' anointing, last supper and prayer in Gethsemane (14.1-42); his arrest and the disciples' flight (14.43-52); Peter's denials and the interrogations of Jesus by the religious leaders and Pilate (14.53–15.20); Jesus' condemnation, crucifixion, death and burial (15.21-47).

Mark's passion account has several striking features, including two instances of the Markan "sandwich" technique, a procedure whereby he interprets a narrative by locating it within two halves of another story.

For example, the generosity of the woman anointing the head of Jesus with costly nard (equal to a year's wages) is contrasted with the grudging complaints of the bystanders about the "waste" involved and, especially, with the grasping outlook of Judas (14.3-9). His treachery made possible the plot against Jesus (14.1-2, 10-11).

Likewise, Peter's cowardice in denying Jesus three times to save his own skin (14.53, 66-72) stands in marked contrast with Jesus' bold declaration of his identity before the high priest and council, leading to his death (14.54-65).

Other prominent features of Mark's narrative are his account of Jesus' prayer in Gethsemane and on the cross. Jesus' twofold petition made known both his felt desire ("for you all things are possible: remove this cup from me") and submission to the divine will ("yet, not what I want, but what you want" [14.36]). It serves as a model for the prayer of disciples. Christians are both bold enough to declare openly their desires, yet humble enough to echo Jesus' instruction to pray "your will be done" (cf. Matthew 6.10; 26.42).

The shocking words of Jesus from the cross, "My God, my God, why have you forsaken me?" (15.34) may be understood in a similar light. Out of his brokenness on the cross, Jesus stays in communion with the Father, making known the state of his soul. The fact that in his extremity Jesus prayed a hymn (Psalm 22) shows disciples the value of fixed prayer forms when they cannot find words to pray.

The confident conclusion of Psalm 22, with its promise to praise God in the people's assembly for rescue from distress, points to Jesus' confident hope that the Father would rescue him out of death's grasp.

Jesus' loud cry signalled his death ("then Jesus gave a loud cry and breathed his last" [15.37]). It was accompanied by two events: the notice about the Temple veil being torn in two, and the Gentile centurion's confession: "truly this man was God's Son!" [15.39]. The torn veil has been interpreted as a sign that God would no longer be present in the Temple or that through the death of Jesus there is now open access to God's presence. For those who accept it, the broken body of Jesus points out that it is by accepting the cross in one's life that the new life of the risen Lord Jesus can be shared.

Easter and the empty tomb

Mark's Gospel ends in puzzling fashion with his account of the discovery of the empty tomb. Mark says the faithful women who went to anoint Jesus' body "fled from the tomb, for terror and amazement had seized them; and they said nothing to anyone, for they were afraid" (16.8).

If, as I believe, this is how Mark's Gospel ended – without resurrection appearances – it leaves readers wondering how the gospel message of Jesus' resurrection became known. (Other endings were added later, including the canonical conclusion [16.9-20].)

Mark's abrupt ending challenges people to make a personal decision regarding the truth implied by the discovery of the empty tomb. Other explanations for the empty tomb – the disciples stole the body and perpetrated a hoax in proclaiming the resurrection, or someone else took the body of Jesus away – must yield to the Christian conviction that Jesus has risen from the dead.

Christian readers believe the Good News that Jesus rose from the dead "on the third day". They have heard, too, that the apostles proclaimed the gospel and some were martyred for the faith. Christians understand that what Jesus had promised the night before he died had truly come to pass ("after I am raised up, I will go before you to Galilee" [14.28]). Jesus reunited his followers in Galilee and sent them on mission.

Perhaps the open-ended conclusion to Mark's Gospel should be seen, then, as an invitation to readers to believe the message of the resurrection. Christians must imagine themselves being called by Christ today to put into action in their lives their belief in a Lord who is simultaneously the crucified ("you are looking for Jesus of Nazareth, who was crucified") and risen Lord ("he has been raised" [16.6]).

Life in the Church

Christians live between the Easter proclamation and the return of Christ in glory to bring all things to their consummation. Mark actually gives his readers an impression of how that is to be for them in Jesus' eschatological address (13.5-37).

Because Jesus uses biblical images about the end times, the truths he communicates are simultaneously revealed in generalities while remaining concealed in their particularity.

All is really left in God's hands. As Jesus says, "about that day or hour no one knows, neither the angels in heaven, nor the Son, but only the Father". Through the centuries, this saying has troubled disciples who believe it is not fitting that Jesus be ignorant of the End. But this statement is deeply reassuring when prophecies of impending doom and gloom surface, as they have been doing with the cyclical presentation of schemes for the end of the world, such as the conclusion of the Mayan calendar in late 2012.

Some people will be tempted to put an ominous spin on the number of deadly earthquakes or other recent natural disasters to draw false conclusions about the end of the world. All such events deserve to be discounted as pointers to the end of history, though they should invite reflection on one's need to be ready at all times for the Lord's coming.

In fact, for the believer, the injunction that Jesus gives at the end of the apocalyptic discourse (13.3-37), "what I say to you I say to all: Keep awake", loses none of its urgency. It encourages Christians to face the future with serenity, putting aside all anxiety about the coming of the Son of Man, Jesus, who is the Lord of history.

Jesus' parable of the master absent "on a journey" and its associated sayings is meant to engender hope. For during his absence, he has put "his slaves in charge" (13.34).

Seeing Jesus in the absent lord and themselves in the servants ("each with a particular task"), Christians delight that they have been entrusted with responsibility for safeguarding his church ("the house").

Disciples should not be led into misguided enthusiasm or become carelessly indifferent. Rather, they should "keep alert ... keep awake", ready to greet Christ whenever he returns from his presence at the right hand of the Father, whether, making reference to the Roman manner of reckoning time, he comes "in the evening, or at midnight, or at cockcrow, or at dawn" (13.35).

III. Preparing for Sunday Mass

Each homilist, study group or other interpreters of the Sunday Scriptures (such as those engaged in handling children's worship) will devise their own appropriate manner of using this book. The following may help those looking for a methodology.

The most important starting point is to read through the gospel and then the first reading several times, looking for common and differing emphases as well as any structural features that stand out.

A second point would be to list problem areas in interpretation. In the texts, what matters or issues are found that contemporary readers may not understand or might struggle with?

At this time, one could read the reflections on the readings to see what clarifications are offered. As each text is very brief (around 700 words), it is not likely that every difficulty will be resolved. Here we see the importance of having access to a biblical commentary or biblical dictionary. I have often found that commentators touch on every issue except the one that interests me; hence the need for several other tools.

Next, the second reading could be read meditatively with the same pattern used in contemplating the gospel and first reading. Because all the texts for solemnities, Advent and Lent are chosen in function of the feast or liturgical season, on those occasions the second reading will more generally fit with the gospel and first reading than would be the case in the Sundays of Ordinary Time or in the Easter season, when the second readings are continuous.

Finally, the psalm could be prayed as a closing devotional exercise that picks up a theme of the Sunday.

May Mary, Mother of the Word Incarnate, who remains for the Church the model for believers who strive to "hear the word of God and obey it" (Luke 11.28), intercede for all who will use this book to deepen their knowledge of God's self-communication in his holy Word.

First Sunday of Advent

God Is Faithful

* Isaiah 63.16b-17, 19; 64.1, 3-8
* Psalm 80
* 1 Corinthians 1.3-9
* Mark 13.33-37

Today begins the liturgical season of Advent, a term that means "arrival" or "coming". In this four-week period, Christians recall the first coming of Christ in his incarnation at Christmas and anticipate his final coming in glory at the end of time.

Advent also joyfully celebrates Christ's daily coming – during the time of the Church – in word and sacrament. The season's purple colour symbolizes hope, a yearning by God's people and all creation for the transforming light of Christ.

Before December 17, the emphasis of the Advent prayers is on the Lord's second coming – his Parousia – which is highlighted on this First Sunday of Advent.

From December 17 through December 25, the focus of the believer's prayer and inner life is the joy of Christmas.

The focus of the Fourth Sunday is the Blessed Virgin Mary, whose openness to God's will models every Christian's response.

On the Second and Third Sundays, John the Baptist's preaching is evoked. As the herald of Christ's coming in the historical public ministry, he pointed to purification from sin and humility of heart as the requisite sentiments to receive Christ whenever he comes.

In telling the Jesus story to encourage the Christians of his day, the evangelist Mark struck a delicate balance between reminding them of the original disciples' weaknesses and reassuring them of their call to service. At the end of the apocalyptic discourse (Mark 13.1-37), Jesus exhorted each of his disciples to be vigilant rather than asleep: "What I say to you I say to all: Keep awake".

Jesus not only urged his disciples on, he entrusted to them his *exousia*. This word has a double meaning: both the task itself and the charge, authority or power needed to fulfill the task: "It is like a man going on a journey, when he leaves home and puts his slaves in charge, each with a particular task".

The power – which each member of Christ's household has been given to carry out his or her task or mission in life – derives from Jesus' own Holy Spirit. Willingly, Christ entrusts power on those who are open to receiving the gifts of the Spirit.

The manner in which Christians carry out their tasks, their mission in life, as they wait for the Son of Man to come, underlies Paul's prayer of thanksgiving, uttered in the opening verses of his First Letter to the Corinthians.

Paul makes three points. First, God is the source of the gifts with which the church at Corinth is endowed. Second, Christian existence is set within an eschatological framework, oriented to the "day of our Lord Jesus Christ". Finally, in the interim between Christ's resurrection and Parousia, God calls disciples to "fellowship" -- life in community with Christ and each other.

The many gifts of "speech and knowledge" became a source of boasting, then division, at Corinth. Paul reminded them that their charisms were gifts of God, to be received with thanksgiving and willingly put at the service of God's people.

Though the community had been richly blessed, Paul told them that they had not yet experienced what the church earnestly longed for: the revealing (*apocalypsis*) of Jesus – his final appearance to triumph over the powers of evil and death (cf. 1 Corinthians 15.20-28, 50-58).

During this time of waiting, Christians must humbly allow themselves to be strengthened by Christ. For his day will be one of judgment, but his grace will render them "blameless". Christians may be hopeful, because, as Paul reassures them, "God is faithful".

God's fidelity becomes manifest here and now in the fellowship or "communion" (*koinonia*) to which the Corinthians are called. This communion refers to the intimate relationship Christians enjoy both with Christ and with one another.

Such fellowship was a radically distinctive characteristic of the early Christian church. Believers were called to share close and sacrificial relationships with those of other social classes with whom they might otherwise have nothing in common.

The new reality of the church uncovers the answer to the spiritual impoverishment that led Isaiah to beg God to "tear open the heavens and come down". Isaiah trusted God, who had acted formerly as Israel's redeemer, to be revealed as Father, creator and renewer of the people. This Advent hope finds its true realization at Christmas.

Second Sunday of Advent

Why Confess One's Sins Today?

* Isaiah 40.1-5, 9-11
* Psalm 85
* 2 Peter 3.8-14
* Mark 1.1-8

Last week, Jesus spoke about the end of time as we know it: his coming in glory as the Son of Man. This week we hear of the "beginning of the good news of Jesus Christ, the Son of God".

The opening to Mark's Gospel consists of one long sentence, with words drawn from Isaiah and Malachi, telling about John the Baptizer appearing in the desert of Judea, near Jerusalem. John was enormously popular ("people from the whole Judean countryside and all the people of Jerusalem were going out to him"), a fire-and-brimstone preacher. He dressed oddly and ate a peculiar diet.

In Mark, John's only recorded words have to do not with himself but with his successor. Though the Baptist immersed the repentant in water, he foretold that someone "more powerful than I" would come later and baptize his hearers "with the Holy Spirit". When speaking of the "one who was coming after him", John spoke humbly, saying, "I am not worthy to stoop down and untie the thong of his sandals".

God's herald, John was a person of great magnetism. His ministry had a tremendous impact. But he paled in comparison with the greatness achieved by Jesus, whose personality and ministry far surpassed his own.

We are told that John preached a "baptism of repentance for the forgiveness of sins" and that the people coming to him for baptism were engaged in "confessing their sins". This happened in reply to John's invitation to "prepare the way of the Lord (= Jesus), make his paths straight".

When the text cited by John was originally proclaimed by Isaiah, it told of God's coming into the wilderness to bring the Jewish people home from the Exile. The early Christians for whom Mark wrote, however, understood Isaiah's words to refer to Jesus. And the exile from which Jesus would release people is alienation from God because of sin.

Though the Dead Sea community – the Essenes of Qumran near where the Baptist preached – also practised ritual washings, their ablutions were repeated, whereas John's immersion occurred only once. The ceremony he performed either expressed their repentance or conveyed God's forgiveness and cleansing to the penitent. The water ritual was understood to be effective only when the convert was truly contrite.

This call to repent now extends to Christians. Indeed, the gospel call to repent of post-baptismal sins has echoed throughout the ages and has led to various confessional practices in different eras. Lent and, to a lesser degree, Advent are liturgical seasons favouring the confession of one's sins, celebrating with the Sacrament of Reconciliation.

Though some wish for a wider use of the Third Rite of Reconciliation, a celebration that concludes with general absolution, church legislation makes clear that this rite is to be used only in extraordinary circumstances. When general absolution is given, it should always be understood that those who receive it have an obligation, as soon as possible afterwards, to make a normal, integral and individual confession of serious sins before celebrating general absolution again. The intention to do this must be present in each individual for general absolution to be effective.

More common in our day are the celebration of the First Rite (which involves individual personal confession) and the Second Rite, a communal celebration of the sacrament during which several priests hear the confessions of penitents.

Confession, we know, has tremendous therapeutic value, even for lesser sins. This fact is recognized even by secular society. An honest statement of how someone has offended God and others is one of the keys to the success of Alcoholics Anonymous and other groups based on the twelve steps.

But much more important is the fact that the Sacrament of Reconciliation allows Jesus, the Good Shepherd, to meet each member of his flock. As the "stronger one", he gladly shares with them his victory over sin, which he won when he gave his life as "a ransom for many" (Mark 10.45; 14.25). This victory is poured out today on individual penitents as the expression of God's compassion and forgiving love.

Each believer has the right to meet Christ, the Divine Physician of souls. Advent, the Church suggests, is a good time for a yearly spiritual check-up, the minimum for Catholics who wish to grow in the spiritual life.

John the Baptist Witnesses to Jesus

* Isaiah 61.1-2a, 10-11
* Luke 1.46-50, 53-54
* 1 Thessalonians 5.16-24
* John 1.6-8, 19-28

The image of John the Baptist in the Synoptic Gospels (Matthew, Mark and Luke) reveals him as an ascetical preacher of repentance. As we saw in last week's gospel passage, "John the Baptist appeared in the wilderness, proclaiming a baptism of repentance for the forgiveness of sins" (Mark 1.4).

The Baptist made his own Isaiah's message to "prepare the way of the Lord, make his paths straight" (Mark 1.3). To all intents and purposes, John wore the mantle of the returning Elijah, whom people expected as the forerunner of God's Messiah. John even replicated Elijah's dress ("John was clothed with camel's hair, with a leather belt around his waist" [Mark 1.6; cf. 2 Kings 1.8]).

Studying the figure of John the Baptist in the Fourth Gospel (the Gospel of John), we find a different portrait of the precursor of Jesus. There the Baptist does not speak of God's imminent final coming for judgment.

As well, in John's Gospel, John the Baptist denied that he was the Messiah ("Who are you?" ... "I am not the Messiah") or Elijah ("What then? Are you Elijah?" He said, "I am not") or the expected prophet like Moses mentioned in Deuteronomy 18.15 ("Are you the Prophet?" He answered, "No.").

The Gospel of John strips the Baptist of all titles – even the designation "the Baptist" – except that of witness to Jesus. John was "a man sent from God" whose sole purpose was to serve "as a witness to testify to the light".

The evangelist pointedly stated that John "was not the light, but he came to testify to the light" – to Jesus, who, later in the gospel, would reveal himself as the "light of the world" (John 8.12). From the start, the Baptist's purpose is clearly enunciated: "so that all might believe through him".

In a passage that appears just beyond the conclusion of today's gospel reading, John gave testimony about the baptism of Jesus: "I saw the Spirit descending from heaven like a dove, and remain on him. I myself did not know him, but the one who sent me to baptize with water said to me, 'He on whom you see the Spirit descend and remain is the one who baptizes with the Holy Spirit'" (John 1.32-33).

After receiving John's denials that he was a messianic figure, the religious authorities sent from Jerusalem inquired about the reasons for his ministry ("Why then are you baptizing if you are neither the Messiah, nor Elijah, nor the Prophet?"). In his answer, John shifted the focus away from baptism to the person for whom he was preparing ("I baptize with water. Among you stands one whom you do not know, the one who is coming after me; I am not worthy to untie the thong of his sandal").

John's humility in his declaration of a subsidiary position in relation to his successor becomes evident when we realize that in the ancient world, not even slaves were obliged to untie the thongs of their masters' sandals.

A later statement of John's summed up his relationship to Jesus. It is one that we as Jesus' disciples might make our own in the Advent season as we seek to bear witness to Jesus in today's world: "he must increase, but I must decrease" (John 3.30).

The opening reading, from Isaiah, foretells the ministry of Jesus, the one on whom, according to John the Baptist's testimony, God's Spirit came to rest: "to bring good news to the oppressed, to bind up the brokenhearted, to proclaim liberty to the captives, and release to the prisoners; to proclaim the year of the Lord's favour".

The joy that God is constantly accomplishing in his people through the Messiah is likened to the joy of a wedding ("as a bridegroom decks himself with a garland and as a bride adorns herself with jewels").

For God causes righteousness and praise to flourish in the world as surely as a garden brings forth new shoots in the spring.

The themes of the selection from Paul's First Letter to the Thessalonians are varied: not quenching the Spirit or despising the words of the prophets. Perhaps the reason for its inclusion in today's liturgy, however, lies in Paul's exhortation to "rejoice always".

This day has long been known as *Gaudete* or "Rejoicing" Sunday. Christians rejoice today because the joy of Christmas is only a few days away.

Fourth Sunday of Advent

God Comes Mysteriously Through Mary's "Yes"

* 2 Samuel 7.1-5, 8b-12, 14a, 16
* Psalm 89
* Romans 16.25-27
* Luke 1.26-38

The wider context of today's first reading contains an elaborate play on the Hebrew word for "house". It means a "palace" (in verse 1); a "dwelling" (in verses 2, 5, 6, 7); a "temple" (in verse 13) and a "royal dynasty" (in verses 11 and 16).

The passage attempts to explain why the Jerusalem Temple was not built by King David but by his son Solomon. More importantly, it communicates how God takes the initiative to encounter humanity – not principally by means of a shrine, but in a person, David's heir.

In this text, the Lord effected a personal covenant with the house of David, replacing direct rule over Israel by rule through a king. Chosen by God, kings in the Davidic succession were to occupy the throne in Israel forever ("your house and your kingdom shall be made sure forever before me").

ARCHBISHOP TERRENCE PRENDERGAST

But when the kingship died out around the time of Israel's exile in Babylon, reflection on God's promise led to hope for another anointed like the king, the "Messiah", who could fulfill God's saving intention.

The unfolding of God's saving plan gets elaborated in as unassuming a manner as God's taking of David from pasturing sheep to shepherding Israel. From Luke's narrative we get the impression of God's eye sweeping over the world until it lighted on a tiny village in Galilee, Nazareth, and focused in on a virgin engaged to a man named Joseph, who, we are told simply, was "of the house of David".

In the rhythm of the text, we sense the angel coming to Mary.

The words Luke used to describe the divine-human encounter through the angel Gabriel echo scriptural messages of the past. "Hail, full of grace! The Lord is with you" recalls the words of Hannah, the prophet Samuel's mother (1 Samuel 1.18) and those of the angel to God's servant Gideon (Judges 6.12).

Mary – as with others whom God had called – experienced confusion and fear ("she was much perplexed by his words and pondered what sort of greeting this might be"). The angelic reassurance ("Do not be afraid, Mary, for you have found favour with God") immediately led to Gabriel's revelation of God's purpose ("you will conceive in your womb and bear a son, and you will name him Jesus").

God's design, Mary and the gospel's readers learn, was to fulfill the promise to David in a way that was scarcely imaginable. The child this country girl is to bear "will be great, and will be called the Son of the Most High, and the Lord God will give to him the throne of his father David".

God's promise to David would come about not by means of an earthly, political reign but in a spiritual dominion without end.

Mary's reply is reminiscent of Zechariah's question when John the Baptist's birth was announced. Whereas Zechariah's response suggested doubt regarding God's plan, Mary's query was guileless and fully in keeping with faith in God. She declared simply that she had not had sexual relations with a man.

The angel replied – equally straightforwardly – that her child would be begotten through the Holy Spirit's overshadowing ("therefore the child to be born will be holy; he will be called Son of God").

Besides giving her the news about her child, Gabriel offered Mary another sign of God's activity in the world: the joy of her relative Elizabeth. Formerly barren into old age, she also had conceived a son. This event stands as proof that "nothing will be impossible with God".

In the closing words of his magisterial letter to the Romans, Paul reflected on the fulfillment of God's promise through the birth of Jesus and his subsequent passion, death and resurrection: "the mystery that was kept secret for long ages ... is now disclosed, and through the prophetic writings is made known to all the Gentiles, according to the command of the eternal God".

In light of this revelation, humanity is not to stand back, indifferent to God's action but, Paul says, is called to "the obedience of faith".

In other words, all in their own circumstances and manner of life are to say – as Mary did in hers – "Here am I, the servant of the Lord; let it be done to me according to your word".

The Holy Family of Jesus, Mary and Joseph

The Radiant Glory of the Lord

* Genesis 15.1-6; 17.3b-5, 15-16; 21.1-7
* Psalm 105
* Hebrews 11.8, 11-12, 17-19
* Luke 2.22-40

The feast of the Holy Family this year places young and old in close proximity, inviting Christian reflection on the sacredness of life from conception to death.

In the Old Testament reading, a selection of passages from several chapters of Genesis, we meet Abram and Sarai. The life of this

ARCHBISHOP TERRENCE PRENDERGAST

elderly couple appeared to be without meaning because they were childless. Abram lamented his family's sorry state and the fact that his inheritance would likely pass to his servant ("O Lord God, what will you give me, for I continue childless, and the heir of my house is Eliezer of Damascus?")

God entered the scene with a renewed promise to Abram and his wife of offspring impossible to count – as numerous as the stars in the heavens ("the father of a multitude of nations"). Making a solemn covenant with this Bedouin couple, God symbolized the change about to take place in their lives by giving them new names.

"Abram" is thought to mean "the [or my] father is exalted". "Abraham" is interpreted to mean "father of a multitude of nations" ("your name shall be Abraham; for I have made you the father of a multitude of nations").

The sacred author gives no etymology of Sarai or Sarah – both seem to be variants of a Semitic word meaning "princess" – but the change of name is symbolic, indicating a special destiny ("I will bless her, and moreover I will give you a son by her ... and she shall give rise to nations; kings of peoples shall come from her").

The reading from Hebrews points to faith as the interpretive principle for all the incidents that involved God in the lives of Abraham and Sarah. Faith is said to have led Abraham to leave his ancestral home and go to the land of promise pointed out by God. Faith underlay Sarah's conception of her child, Isaac, despite her old age ("by faith Sarah herself, though barren, received power to conceive").

In the gospel, Luke tells of a profound encounter between the child Jesus and an elderly couple in the Jerusalem Temple. It was a moment that prophetically anticipated future occasions when people would make Jesus the focal point of their conversations.

Simeon foresaw those future meetings as occasions in which some would reject Jesus, while others would receive him ("This child is destined for the falling and rising of many in Israel, and to be a sign that will be opposed"). It would be a moment so poignant as to pierce any mother's heart – especially Mary's ("and a sword will pierce your own soul too").

For this fleeting moment, though, Jesus brought deep joy and consolation into the hearts of many who heard of the happening, but especially to the elders Simeon and Anna, who had shared in the joyous moment. For them it became a moment of sheer liberation!

In Jesus' "presentation" in the Temple we see Jesus bringing fulfillment to faithful Jews, who are the descendants of Abraham and Sarah, prototypes of all who believe in God. Formerly centred on the Temple, the long yearned-for renewal of Israel's worship finds embodiment in the person of Jesus.

Once they have met Jesus, Simeon and Anna face their imminent deaths with peace. Simeon can confidently sing his *Nunc dimittis* ("now you are dismissing your servant in peace, according to your word") – the hymn the Church prays each evening at Compline – and Anna's long wait finds her expectations fulfilled in Jesus.

Their eyes have seen a hint of the coming glory of the Lord, a foretaste of the Risen One's new and eternal life. Now they can look forward to death unafraid and filled with joy ("for my eyes have seen your salvation").

Though Simeon foresees suffering in the futures of Mary and Jesus, the Holy Spirit also moves him to foretell the glory of Jesus' resurrection, which overcomes the shame of the cross. Simeon calls Jesus "a light" enlightening the Gentiles and the "glory" of Israel.

Anna, besides being a model of faithful waiting for God's promises to be fulfilled, also illustrates the truth that once a person has encountered Jesus, they can't help but tell others about him ("she came, and began to speak about the child to all who were looking for the redemption of Jerusalem").

Epiphany of the Lord

Honouring God's Anointed King

* Isaiah 60.1-6
* Psalm 72

* Ephesians 3.2-3a, 5-6
* Matthew 2.1-12

The readings for the Epiphany of the Lord contrast a program for the ideal ruler of Israel with the despicable behaviour of King Herod, who appears in the second chapter of Matthew's Gospel as paranoid, duplicitous and cruel.

Psalm 72 was probably composed for use at the coronation of the Davidic kings. The verbs used to describe the king's actions may be interpreted as indicatives (the New International Version reads "he will rule from sea to sea") or as hortatory imperatives (the New Revised Standard Version has instead "may he have dominion from sea to sea").

Used at the king's enthronement, the psalm may have functioned as both a charge to him and a prayer for his reign.

The key concepts for God's rule – which the king was bound to enact – are "justice" and "righteousness", words found in the opening verses. The chiastic (inverted) arrangement of the first two verses has the effect of surrounding both king and people with God's justice.

Typically, such justice becomes manifest towards "your poor". Indeed, the king's one responsibility mentioned in the first seven verses is to "defend the cause of the poor of the people, give deliverance to the needy, and crush the oppressor".

Such a governmental program would make "righteousness flourish and peace abound". Therein also lies the cause of the "prosperity" that both mountains and hills were urged to yield. After describing such an ideal, the psalmist waxes eloquent, suggesting that such a king should rule not only "from sea to sea" but "to the ends of the earth".

Scholars are uncertain whether "the River" refers to the great river Euphrates or to the mythical river that was believed to flow out from God's throne in Jerusalem. Mention of other geographic places such as Tarshish (in Spain), the Isles (either Mediterranean locales or symbolizing distant places) and Sheba and Seba (the Arabian peninsula) imagines the king's sovereignty as embracing the whole world, its rulers and peoples ("may all kings fall down before him, all nations give him service").

The disparity between this vision of a worldwide social order embodying justice and compassion ("For he delivers the needy one who calls, the poor and the one who has no helper. He has pity on the weak and the needy, and saves the lives of the needy"), and what the kings of Israel actually delivered, led to the psalm being interpreted messianically.

Biblical faith held that sometime – in a future God would determine – these ideals would be realized.

Trito- (the Third) Isaiah saw the imminent fulfillment of the psalmist's vision taking place during the restoration of God's people after the exile. He foresaw Israel, now gathered from distant lands, on the cusp of a new era when the wealth of the world ("gold and frankincense") would flow into Jerusalem. Then foreign kings would serve in Zion ("Nations shall come to your light, and kings to the brightness of your dawn").

Isaiah therefore exuberantly urged Jerusalem to "Arise, shine!" For God was at work within the Holy City, radiating his dazzling presence.

The Christian community of believers understood such prophecies – found scattered through Isaiah and other scriptures – to have been accomplished in Jesus' life, death and resurrection. In Ephesians, Paul explained that this truth, though "not made known to humankind" in former ages, had become known to him "by revelation".

However, in being fulfilled, the former expectations have undergone transformation. Formerly the nations would have been seen as becoming subservient to God's people. Instead, in the Christian interpretation, God has chosen to put the nations on an equal footing with Israel ("the Gentiles have become fellow heirs, members of the same body [= the Church], and sharers in the promise in Christ Jesus through the Gospel").

The Magi ("wise men from the East") anticipate, during the infancy of Jesus, the coming of the Gentiles to faith in Jesus. Christians of all ages have made their own the obeisance offered to the Christ child ("they knelt down and paid him homage").

If they truly wish to honour "the child who has been born king of the Jews", disciples today would make their own the program of Christ, sharing his vision of a world of equality and justice, of compassion, love and peace.

The Baptism of the Lord

Solidarity with God's Anointed Son

* Isaiah 55.1-11
* Isaiah 12
* 1 John 5.1-9
* Mark 1.7-11

During my first stay in Israel, I experienced an occasional sense of disorientation. Whether I rode a bus, walked through Old Jerusalem or visited one of the holy places, I seemed to be encountering the same Hasidic Jew.

Only after some time did I realize that these devotees of the Torah so completely adhered to similar traditions that, to an outsider, they seemed identical. In addition to wearing the same religious symbols, they were alike in the way they walked, how they talked, even how they held a cigarette!

Likely they were followers of a particular rabbinical tradition. Perhaps they were even disciples of the same master. By a common manner of life and religious devotion, they were set apart from others, including their fellow Jews.

In a way, Our Lord, in today's gospel, takes the opposite tack. Though set apart from others in his unique divine Sonship and sinlessness, he joined with sinful people as they drew near John the Baptist in repentance. Jesus' solidarity with them in yearning for the renewal of God's covenant was the occasion for the Father to delight in his beloved Son.

In Mark's Gospel, John the Baptist's preaching constituted the beginning of the Good News about Jesus Christ the Son of God (cf. Mark 1.1, 4). His proclamation was of a baptism of repentance for the forgiveness of sins (Mark 1.4), which fulfilled God's prophecies in the past (1.2-3).

John confessed that he was an unworthy servant of the coming one, testifying, in fact, that his water baptism was a mere shadow of the baptism with the Holy Spirit that Jesus would confer (Mark 1.8).

In the centuries before Jesus, Israel had reckoned the time of prophecy over and the heavens shut up for good. By declaring the heavens "torn apart" at Jesus' baptism, however, Mark graphically described the ushering in of a new era.

In Mark's narrative (unlike what we find in Matthew's account), the Father's revelation is given to Jesus personally ("You are my Son, the beloved; with you I am well pleased"). This text is a variant of God's word to the specially chosen servant (Isaiah 42.1).

In this extraordinary event at the Jordan, one may see the fulfillment not only of Isaiah's prophecy concerning the servant of the Lord, called to "bring forth justice to the nations", but also of God's invitation – which Isaiah expressed – to "come to the waters" for divine refreshment.

While eating and drinking imply lavish feasting ("delight yourselves in rich food"), the prophet actually intended that his listeners feast on the teaching God offers ("Incline your ear, and come to me; listen so that you may live").

God's wisdom, we learn, differs totally from the way humans see things ("as the heavens are higher than the earth, so are my ways than your ways and my thoughts than your thoughts").

The only way forward lies by way of conversion – that repentance called for by John the Baptist (or, as Isaiah says, "let the wicked person forsake their way, and the unrighteous person their thoughts"). Even if the scope of this enterprise seems hopeless, Isaiah argued that one may take hope from God's nature and the promise that his Word would as surely fulfill its purpose as snow and rain draw forth from the earth a fruitful harvest.

Following Christ's death and resurrection, the evangelist John declares in his First Letter that adherence to God's Word consists in believing "that Jesus is the Christ". This leads the believer to be "born [as a child] of God".

When St. John mentioned that Jesus came "not with the water only but with the water and the blood", he linked Jesus' disposition at his baptism ("the water") to his mind at the crucifixion ("the blood"). By this John undermined the view of a few Christian dissidents who gloried in the theophany at Jesus' baptism but despised the shame of his crucifixion.

Through their baptism, Christians have experienced a reverse solidarity with Jesus. Though sinners, they are made holy in him. They express that solidarity with Jesus not in the way they dress or look, but in their inner attitude of humble service – which reflects his own.

Disciples live out this attitude, as Jesus did, in compassionate service of others. His solidarity with sinners gets transformed into their solidarity with him, God's chosen one.

Second Sunday in Ordinary Time

What Is Implied in Being Called by God?

* 1 Samuel 3.3b-10, 19
* Psalm 40
* 1 Corinthians 6.13c-15a, 17-20
* John 1.35-42

All three readings today involve the notion of call. However, this call is more evident in the vocation of Samuel and in the invitation Jesus gives two inquirers to "Come and see" than it is in Paul's invitation to "glorify God in your body".

Paul's First Letter to the Corinthians challenges social conventions: not only those of the first-century society in which he lived, but those of our time, too.

The Apostle's argument is a little difficult to follow, because Greek manuscripts had no punctuation, let alone quotation marks. Matters are not made easier by the fact that the lectionary reading begins in mid-verse and then drops a verse and half in the middle of Paul's exposition!

In his presentation, Paul made use of the Greek diatribe style of rhetorical discourse. He cited statements current in the Church at Corinth, then gave his own view, usually a refutation or correction.

For example, many scholars believe the first part of this discussion began with Paul quoting a Corinthian slogan about Christian freedom, "All things are lawful for me", which he qualified with the rejoinder, "but not all things are beneficial" (6.12).

The argumentation is not always clear, since at times it is not evident where Corinthian positions begin or end and where Paul's remarks come into play. However, I find the following reconstruction by Richard B. Hayes (*Interpretation Commentary*, 1997, p. 105) plausible.

Paul: "Flee fornication!"

Corinthians [objecting]: ["But why?] Every sin a person commits is outside the body."

Paul: "But the fornicator sins against his own body."

The "enlightened" Corinthian Christians were saying that, because of Christ's resurrection, bodily actions were of no significance. Paul objected, saying that, by linking his body with a prostitute, a fornicator sinned against his own body. His actions hurt not only the Church but also himself. This was tragic because each individual Christian's body is a temple of the Holy Spirit.

In other places, Paul had used the temple imagery in reference to the whole Christian community. Here he transfers the metaphor to each individual disciple of Jesus.

Earlier on, Paul had charged the Church with the task of purifying itself by casting out a man who was living in an incestuous relationship with his stepmother (5.1-13). Now Paul says that each individual's body should be kept as a disciplined holy vessel fit for the Spirit, who dwells in the believer.

This section ends with a reiteration of the notion that each person's body is not the individual's personal property, to do with as he or she pleases. Paul insisted that by the ransom from bondage to sin achieved for each person by Christ's death on the cross, "you are not your own ... you were bought with a price".

In this passage, Paul moves regularly from a declaration about what God in Christ has achieved for the Christian (the indicative) to how the individual must now live (the imperative). For example, Paul does not say that one should keep the body holy so that God may offer you the Spirit, but rather, because the Holy Spirit already dwells in you, you should keep your body from fornication.

Today, fornication as a sin committed by an individual with a prostitute is still an affliction of society. It is also the objective description of those who engage in sexual activity outside marriage and those who cohabit without benefit of marriage. As such, and in a change from past experience, it has become widespread in society, even among Catholics.

The negative effects of this situation were published in a report by the United States Bishops' Committee on Marriage and Family: "Cohabitation as a permanent or temporary alternative to marriage is a major factor in the declining centrality of marriage in family structure. It is a phenomenon altering the face of family life in first-world countries" (*Origins* 29:14 [September 16, 1999], p. 215).

Today, the Church needs to engage this issue of sexual morality as Paul did the views of the Corinthians. The challenge is to help disciples see that "remaining with Jesus" today, as Andrew and his companion once did, involves embracing Jesus' views – communicated by the Church – on the major issues of life. Christians need to say of God's designs, as Samuel did, "Speak, Lord, for your servant is listening!"

Third Sunday in Ordinary Time

God's Transforming Call

* Jonah 3.1-5, 10
* Psalm 25
* 1 Corinthians 7.29-31
* Mark 1.14-20

All three scripture readings introduce us to people who have been called to the special ministry of proclaiming conversion. Though Peter, Andrew, James and John are depicted as immediately leaving trade, possessions and family to follow Jesus unreservedly, the rest of Mark's Gospel shows that they had to struggle before fully accepting the new mindset that Jesus offered them.

Both Jonah and Paul also went through turmoil before they yielded to God's invitation to a change in their way of viewing the world. We must conclude, then, that Jesus' challenge to "repent, and believe in the good news" may be more difficult than it first appears.

On hearing the Jonah story, people tend to focus on the episode in which he was swallowed by a whale and then vomited onto dry land after uttering a prayer of thanksgiving for deliverance. The reason Jonah ended up in the depths of the sea in the first place was that he was fleeing as far as possible from Nineveh after God summoned him to preach judgment and repentance to the citizens of that place.

After Jonah proclaimed repentance and Nineveh repented, Jonah brooded because the effectiveness of God's mercy left his oracle of judgment unfulfilled. Some modern interpreters see the message of Jonah as a plea that Israel never cease to preach to the nations God's universal mercy.

The book also stresses a change in the prophet's role from that of delivering oracles of judgment to one of persuading people to a change of heart. For God's decrees can be reversed through repentance.

In last week's gospel, John the Baptist pointed out Jesus as the "Lamb of God" to Andrew and another disciple. These disciples went to see where Jesus stayed, and accepted him as the Messiah. Andrew then got his brother Simon Peter and brought him to Jesus.

These traditions, found only in John's Gospel, probably reflect the historical connection between Jesus' ministry and that of John the Baptist, which overlapped for a period of time.

When Mark narrates his story of Jesus, he simplifies matters considerably. Once John had been arrested (the Greek verb translated as "arrested" literally means "handed over" and indicates John's death as part of God's plan), Jesus came into Galilee preaching conversion ("repent") as John had done. But Jesus' preaching contained a further appeal to "believe in the good news".

John the Baptist predicted the imminent arrival of one who would baptize with the Spirit. That time had arrived ("The time is fulfilled, and the kingdom of God has come near"). The assertion that the kingdom has "come near" in the preaching of Jesus conceals a tension between the present but hidden fulfillment of God's kingdom in the ministry of Jesus and the kingdom's future completion in power, the focus of Jesus' teaching in parables.

In Jesus' ministry, the kingdom of God has entered into history even though its full appearance is yet to come.

Paul plays on this tension between the "already" and "not yet" dimensions of God's kingdom as it is lived out by disciples. He claims that "the appointed time has grown short" and "the present form of this world is passing away".

Living the Christian life, therefore, is paradoxical ("those who mourn as though they were not mourning, and those who rejoice as though they were not rejoicing, and those who buy as though they had no possessions").

For Jesus' program to become operative, he needed fellow evangelists to spread the good news. In today's gospel he called others to fish for people. This alludes to the former livelihood of four Galileans ("for they were fishermen") and the way in which Jesus transformed their lives by his call ("follow me and I will make you fishers of people").

Jeremiah's similar proclamation – "I am sending for many fishermen, says the Lord, and they shall catch them" (16.16) – focused on God's judgment against evildoers.

By contrast, Jesus summons disciples now, as he did in the past, to rescue the lost and to help in the work of announcing and preparing for the kingdom of God. This remains "good news", even though it continues to demand a change of outlook regarding God's designs and rule, about how the kingdom is present in the world through the Church and on how Jesus' message transforms lives today.

Fourth Sunday in Ordinary Time

Jesus' Teaching 'with Authority' Provokes Wonder

* Deuteronomy 18.15-20
* Psalm 95
* 1 Corinthians 7.32-35
* Mark 1.21-28

Last Sunday's second reading ended with Paul observing that "the present form of this world is passing away". This weekend, a similar note is struck when Paul speaks of the value of celibacy – singleness, being unmarried – so that men and women may be "concerned about the affairs of the Lord".

Paul says this not because, as is sometimes asserted, he has a negative view of sex. His outlook on human sexuality is realistic and positive. He recognizes it as a divine blessing meant to lead to intimacy within marriage.

Beginning his mini-treatise on marriage, divorce and celibacy for the sake of the kingdom (1 Corinthians 7.1-40), Paul told the Corinthians, who thought everyone should be celibate, that, instead, "each man should have his own wife and each woman her own husband.

ARCHBISHOP TERRENCE PRENDERGAST

The husband should give his wife her conjugal rights, and likewise the wife to her husband" (7.2-3).

Later, treating the issue of the single state, Paul praised it for allowing one to serve the Lord without distraction ("the unmarried man is anxious about the affairs of the Lord, how to please the Lord").

On the other hand, Paul said, marriage presents complications, producing divided interests. The married Christian must rightly consider how to please his or her spouse rather than concentrating on pleasing God alone ("the married woman is concerned about the affairs of the world, how to please her husband").

In contrast with our culture, which claims that the unmarried state is unhealthy and that wholeness for humans is possible only through sexual relationships, Paul reminds believers that the single state has dignity and value before God.

Through the ages, the Church has affirmed the truth of what Paul says through admiration for religious life, for the celibacy of priests in the Latin Rite and for disciples who, being single for a variety of motives, thereby can offer "unhindered devotion to the Lord".

There is only one reference in the New Testament to Jesus' celibate state, though it is everywhere presupposed. A single saying of Jesus on this theme has been preserved: "For some are eunuchs because they were born that way; others were made that way by men; and others have renounced marriage because of the kingdom of heaven" (Matthew 19.12; New International Version).

Those "who have made themselves eunuchs for the sake of the kingdom" (New Revised Standard Version) remain celibate to devote themselves fully to Christian ministry or witness. Marriage and the family are highly esteemed by disciples of Jesus. Still, exceptional people of the early community remained unmarried as a mark of their singular calling.

Jesus' single-minded devotion to heralding the kingdom is evident from the outset. Mark's initial description of Jesus' ministry is that it presents "a new teaching – with authority!" The power in his teaching is evident when linked with an exorcism ("He commands even the unclean spirits, and they obey him").

Mark stressed the impact of Jesus' teaching without telling us what feature of it displayed that authority. His focus was on the authority as such and on the people's reaction ("they were astounded"). Or, as translator R. Gundry suggests, "they were being knocked out with astonishment".

Mark wanted to emphasize the overwhelming power of Jesus' teaching authority. As long as Jesus taught, astonishment overwhelmed the residents of Capernaum. Mark thought it unimportant to inform his readers of what Jesus said in his teaching. Instead, Mark showed that the power of Jesus' teaching authority became manifest in his casting "an unclean spirit" out of a man who came into the synagogue of Capernaum.

As Mark's Gospel progresses, readers will observe Jesus working three other exorcisms (Mark 5.1-20; 7.24-30; 9.14-29).

Yet Mark multiplies the impression of the extent of Jesus' exorcising activity through summary statements that generalize this feature of his ministry (cf. 1.34, 39; 3.11-12; 15; 22-23; 6.13; 9.38).

Mark identifies an exorcism as the first of Jesus' mighty acts and links the exorcism to the authoritative teaching of Jesus. The two activities coordinate and support each other, evoking astonishment and causing the fame of Jesus to spread through the surrounding Galilean countryside.

The question that the people of Capernaum asked ("What is this?") will soon become a question dominating the first half of Mark's Gospel: "Who is this?" (4.41). Ultimately, it will become the question Jesus poses to each person: "Who do you say that I am?" (8.29)

Fifth Sunday in Ordinary Time

Healing the Sick, Proclaiming the Message

* Job 7.1-4, 6-7
* Psalm 147

* 1 Corinthians 9.16-19, 22-23
* Mark 1.29-39

One of the most enduring reflections on suffering as an aspect of the human condition is found in the Book of Job. Its readers are faced with a model child of God who, though he has done no wrong, faces extraordinary travails: loss of family, material goods and the reputation of his good name.

Like the person enduring illness and pain, Job lamented, "When I lie down I say, 'When shall I rise?' But the night is long and I am full of tossing until dawn".

Aware of the extent of human suffering all over the world, Blessed Pope John Paul II declared February 11, feast of Our Lady of Lourdes, as the World Day of the Sick. Several years later, the Holy Father wrote an apostolic letter, *Salvifici Doloris*, which drew attention to the "saving dimension of suffering".

In that reflection, the pope underlined the Church's perennial care of the sick in imitation of Jesus. But he went on to stress the contribution that those bound by illness make to the saving power of Jesus when they unite their sufferings with his on the cross.

In a remarkable act of interpretation, Mark described Jesus' healing of a "man with an unclean spirit" in Capernaum as "a new teaching – with authority!"

Today's gospel continues that vision of a ministry that is simultaneously teaching and healing; the gospel offers a glimpse of the extraordinary power Jesus exercised in his public ministry and focused on the healing of Simon Peter's mother-in-law.

Since Mark often depicts Jesus teaching his disciples in the house (cf. 4.10, 34; 7.17), one may be justified in understanding this healing in the house of Simon and Andrew as instruction.

Form critics who have studied the narrative structure of gospel healing stories have isolated a four-part schema: a description of the illness (in this case "fever", understood as an illness rather than as we would today think of fever as a symptom of illness), a request for healing ("they told Jesus about her at once"), the healer's action (literally "seizing her hand"), and proof that the ailing person has been restored to health ("she began to serve them").

Jesus cured Peter's mother-in-law, who had been confined to bed with a fever (caused by malaria, perhaps?), in an instant. "He came and took her by the hand and lifted her up". Fevers may have been associated with demonic possession (in Luke 4.39 – which tells the same story – Jesus "rebuked" the fever). Mark says "the fever left her".

By his arrangement of the cures of a man and a woman, Mark may have wished to highlight the universality of Jesus' healing service. The summary description of the healings that took place at the door to the house after sundown (for people would not have carried the sick until the Sabbath was over) generalizes the preceding episodes: "they brought to Jesus all who were sick or possessed with demons".

Mark offers several such summaries of Jesus' magnetism (cf. 3.7-10; 6.53-56). The impact of Jesus' ministry, even early in his career, may be gauged from Mark's remark that "the whole city was gathered around the door").

Some have emphasized the difference between "all" who came for healing and the "many" whom Jesus cured ("he cured many who were sick with various diseases, and cast out many demons"). Most interpreters, however, see "many" as a Semitic turn of phrase that is the equivalent of "all".

There remain other unexplored features in Mark's early account of Jesus' curative power, such as the importance of faith for healing. Instead, Mark emphasizes Jesus' silencing of the demons (it is possible that, by revealing his identity, they intended to thwart his mission), intimacy with God in prayer, lack of interest in fame, and concern to spread his message "throughout Galilee, proclaiming the message [of the gospel] in their synagogues".

Paul manifested a similar disinterested mindset when he chose to forgo entitlements – such as financial support from his churches – that were rightly his as a minister of the gospel. He declared his motive to be "for the sake of the Gospel, so that I may share in its blessings".

This approach included identifying with those who suffer human frailty in order to bring them to God ("to the weak I became weak, so that I might win the weak").

Sixth Sunday in Ordinary Time

The Messianic Secret in Mark's Gospel

* Leviticus 13.1-2, 45-46
* Psalm 32
* 1 Corinthians 10.31–11.1
* Mark 1.40-45

In the Bible, leprosy describes a whole series of scaly skin diseases. Since "lepers" could contaminate others and make them ritually impure – that is, unable to participate in public worship – people so afflicted had to dress in torn clothing and warn others not to come too close, in the manner described in today's reading from Leviticus.

Given this background, it should not be surprising that the story of the healing of the leper in Mark is full of powerful feelings and hints at underlying issues.

It opens with the leper approaching Jesus as a suppliant ("a man with leprosy came to Jesus begging him, and kneeling said to Jesus, 'If you choose, you can make me clean'"). This is already a powerful confession by the man about Jesus' authority, for Jewish belief held that only God could cleanse a leper or raise the dead.

In reply, Jesus manifested powerful emotions, either "moved with pity", as in our version, or – according to a variant reading – "becoming angry". Though it is attested in only a few manuscripts, some scholars argue that we should read "anger" rather than "compassion", because it is easier to see how "becoming angry" would be changed to "moved with pity" than vice versa.

If anger is chosen as Jesus' emotion, it should be understood as righteous anger, directed against the distortion of God's creature by the forces of evil.

Jesus deliberately stretched out his hand and touched the leper – a very daring action – for ordinarily contact with a leper was thought to transfer uncleanness and was forbidden. Jesus said to him, "I do choose. Be made clean!" The consequence flowed directly from Jesus' touch: "Immediately the leprosy left him [as if it were a power indwelling him], and he was made clean".

Then, Jesus again manifested strong feelings, "sternly warning" the leper to be silent about his cure. The Greek verb means to "snort" or "puff", like a disturbed horse, or as an expression of anger and agitation. One suggestion is that Jesus was making use of oriental sign language, placing his hand on his lips and blowing air in puffs through his teeth, demanding silence: "See that you say nothing to anyone".

Except the healed leper was simultaneously told by Jesus to go to the priests and make an offering in thanksgiving for his healing, as prescribed by Moses. In this way, the leper could be certified for re-entry into the worshipping community and civil society. This action on Jesus' part shows that, though he may criticize the religious leaders' interpretation of God's intent in the scriptures (cf. 2.1–3.6), he also affirmed the enduring value of the Torah when it benefited people.

Jesus' injunction to silence has been seen as a part of the theme of secrecy in Mark's Gospel, at times referred to as the "messianic secret".

Yet, the evidence about this secrecy motif is more complex than first appears. Twice, Jesus commanded the demons to be silent about his identity (1.34; 3.12). Three times, Jesus enjoined silence in a healing context (1.44; 5.43; 7.36) and twice he told the disciples to be quiet: about his identity as messiah (8.30) and about what Peter, James and John had seen on the mount of Transfiguration (9.9).

However, the secrecy motif is absent from several other miracles and, contrary to the pattern, Jesus once told someone (the healed demoniac of Gerasa) to declare in the Decapolis – Gentile territory – "how much the Lord has done for you, and what mercy he has shown you" (5.19).

It seems that Mark offered a key to resolving the tension between secrecy and openness when he noted that Jesus spoke "quite openly" about his coming passion (8.32). Combined with Jesus' demand for silence about his messiahship two verses earlier, this reality may be interpreted in this way: "do not say Jesus is messiah without mentioning his mission to suffer and die for others".

Demons, in revealing Jesus' divine Sonship, sought to deflect him from this destiny. So would focusing on Jesus' miracles without reference to faith's role in healing, or people indiscriminately confessing him as messiah.

Jesus' true mission is hinted at in today's ironic closing verse, where Jesus replaces the leper as the outcast from society ("Jesus could no longer go into a town openly"), which foreshadows the cross.

Seventh Sunday in Ordinary Time

The Son of Man's Authority to Forgive Sins

* Isaiah 43.18-19, 20-22, 24-25
* Psalm 41
* 2 Corinthians 1.18-22
* Mark 2.1-12

Upon examination, the apparently simple structure of Mark's Gospel reveals a series of parallels. One of these distinguishes the Galilean ministry of Jesus from the period of his teaching in Jerusalem. In each phase, we find parables narrated (in Galilee [4.1-34]; in Jerusalem [12.1-12]) and controversies appearing in blocks (in Galilee [2.1–3.6]; in Jerusalem [11.27-33 + 12.13-37]).

Mark, it seems, has arranged blocks of material – shaped by early oral or written traditions – into an engaging narrative about Jesus' path to the cross and resurrection. Whether and how the evangelist might have ordered the internal features of these stories remains an ongoing topic of discussion.

Today's gospel introduces the first of five controversies: the healing of a paralytic, revealing Jesus' authority on earth to forgive sins. Three other controversies (why Jesus' disciples do not fast; Jesus' defence of his disciples for picking heads of grain on the Sabbath; and Jesus' Sabbath cure of the man with a withered hand) will be presented in the coming Sundays.

This first collection of controversial encounters between Jesus and the religious leaders concludes with the ominous notice that the Pharisees began to conspire with the Herodians "how to destroy him" (3.6). It was this assertion by Mark that led the German scholar Martin Kähler to describe Mark's Gospel as a "Passion Narrative with an introduction".

Attentive readers will observe that the removal of verses 5 to 10, which contain the controversy about Jesus' authority to forgive sins, would leave a simple story about Jesus healing a paralytic. Yet it remains problematic to infer that a controversy was later introduced into a healing story.

For, as we have already seen, Jesus healed the sick (1.21-45). And the unit following this story shows Jesus associating with sinners (2.15-17). Jewish traditions associated illness with sin (cf. John 5.14; 9.2; Psalm 103.3) and several prophets foretold that the coming age of salvation would bring healing and forgiveness ("I am about to do a new thing", God declares through Isaiah in today's first reading). So the combination of forgiveness and healing in a single gospel unit, while surprising and infrequent, is understandable.

Jesus began his ministry by proclaiming that the kingdom of God had come, urging people to accept this good news by personal conversion. He then began to attack the powers of demonic possession and sickness by exorcisms and cures. Now, in the cure of a paralytic, Jesus reminds disciples that forgiveness is central to healing.

Contemporary psychoanalysis suggests that deep-seated guilt and self-hatred can become manifest in paralyzing physical symptoms. However one views the link between body and spirit, Jesus presents his ministry as one oriented towards the total healing of each person.

Though the religious leaders consider Jesus' declaration "your sins are forgiven" [by God] to be blasphemy, he gives no reply to this charge. However, when he works the miracle of healing, he asserts a claim to authority over sins on earth, taking a step beyond his initial declaration ("that you may know that the Son of Man has authority on earth to forgive sins").

In offering healing to the paralytic, Jesus referred to himself as "the Son of Man", a title that has been the subject of intense scholarly debate. Such a character ("one like a son of man") appears in Daniel 7.13 as an apocalyptic figure, whereas in Ezekiel it refers to the prophet with his human limitations (leading the New Revised Standard Version to translate the term there as "mortal").

Thus, the designation "Son of Man" – almost always found only on the lips of Jesus – could readily both identify Jesus with human beings and point to his role in God's plans as the end-time messenger appointed to judge the men and women of this world whose condition he shared.

For disciples to whom Jesus today grants forgiveness of sins through his Church in the Sacrament of Reconciliation, this gift is one of consolation and healing. It may help those who struggle with the obligation to confess their sins to another human being to keep in mind that, in the confessor, they meet the "Son of Man" who understands their human condition with its limitations.

Through the priest, Jesus says to them – anticipating their encounter with him at the end of time – "Your sins are forgiven".

Eighth Sunday in Ordinary Time

"New Wine into Fresh Wineskins"

* Hosea 2.14b, 15b, 19-20
* Psalm 103
* 2 Corinthians 3.1-6
* Mark 2.18-22

So far in reading Mark's Gospel, we have seen a new era inaugurated by Jesus' healings, exorcisms and claim to forgive sins. Now readers begin to learn some of the implications for personal piety deriving from the new era of the kingdom of God.

Today Christians are asked to reflect on the attitude they should have towards the practice of fasting found in Christianity, as in Judaism and other religions.

Though fasts might be appropriate in times of national disaster (cf. Isaiah 58.3-6; Esther 4.16), Jewish law obliged fasting on only one day of the year, Yom Kippur – the Day of Atonement (Leviticus 16.1-34; Numbers 29.7-11). Still, fasts could accompany a person's special supplication of God to express mourning or repentance (cf. 1 Kings 21.27; Daniel 9.3; Nehemiah 1.4).

Accordingly, fasting came to be associated in popular piety with prayer and almsgiving, symbolizing the person's yearning to be faithful and righteous. In Jesus' day, the disciples of John the Baptist fasted and some Pharisees are said to have fasted twice a week (cf. Luke 18.12), probably on Mondays and Thursdays, as in rabbinic times.

Yet there were times when fasting was clearly inappropriate. Since fasting was linked with mourning or penitence, guests who came to a marriage in mourning attire or fasting would create a social disturbance and insult their hosts. Their behaviour would intimate that somehow they disapproved of the wedding.

With this in mind, today's gospel unit may be divided into three parts: a saying by Jesus that rejects fasting because his presence must be understood as that of the bridegroom at God's wedding feast; a clarification that fasting would become appropriate for disciples as a response to Jesus' death; and a pair of proverbs about a patch and new wine arguing for the incompatibility of the practice of fasting during Jesus' ministry.

We should presume that the disciples failed to fast because Jesus did not, just as we imagine that John' disciples fasted because the Baptist did. We might see the issue as one of authority, parallelling last week's issue about Jesus' power to forgive sins on earth, and anticipating next week's issue of Jesus' right to modify Sabbath observance. At issue is whether Jesus has the authority to suspend fasting for his disciples when other religious leaders required it of theirs.

In Jesus' cryptic description of himself as "the bridegroom", we have a declaration that his presence brings about an utterly novel time. Fasting belongs to the period before he came and will mark the time after his death ("then they will fast on that day").

In fact, fasting among Jesus' followers would recall his being "taken away", something that, according to the *Didache* – "the Teaching of the Twelve Apostles" – the early Church recalled on Wednesdays and Fridays.

But the time of Jesus' ministry remains utterly unique. Jesus was in a class by himself. His presence and removal determine whether one abstains from fasting or fasts.

A wedding feast calls for good clothes and an abundant supply of wine. So the proverbial sayings – while apparently unconnected – also touch on the presence of the bridegroom. Sometimes they are interpreted as simply telling of the incompatibility of the new and the old (the new patch on the old garment or the new wine that one tries to pour into old wineskins).

But there is more. A new ("unshrunken") cloth will last on an old cloak only until the next washing; then a greater tear results. Old wineskins stretched to their limits can only burst when the new wine ferments and swells within them. With Jesus come irresistible new forces that can do nothing but burst human expectations. The only way of grasping the meaning of Jesus' coming is to have a change of outlook to be able to see that "the new wine" of his presence and the joy it brings require a whole new way of looking at life – "fresh wineskins".

Hosea had a similar vision to effect the reversal of Israel's infidelities. God would again woo the chosen people by recreating their courtship period in the wilderness and thus win back Israel's devotion.

Likewise, Paul described God's new covenant-making activity through Jesus as an inner transformation written now on human hearts, instead of on the stone tablets of Sinai.

Ninth Sunday in Ordinary Time

"Observe the Sabbath Day and Keep It Holy"

* Deuteronomy 5.12-15
* Psalm 81
* 2 Corinthians 4.6-11
* Mark 2.23–3.6

For Judaism, the Sabbath was its most distinctive observance and a matter of national pride. As we read in Deuteronomy, God commanded Israel through Moses to "Observe the Sabbath day and keep it holy".

However, God gave very few specifics about what keeping the Sabbath holy implied, except that it meant not doing any work: "Six days you shall labour and do all your work. But the seventh day ... you shall not do any work".

But what is meant by "work"? And are necessary forms of work forbidden? Such questions regularly occupied Jewish religious thought, gave wide scope for a range of opinions, and help explain today's gospel confrontation between Jesus and his coreligionists.

Since the disappearance in Canada of "blue laws" outlawing recreational and work-associated activities (except church) on Sunday, the Christian "Sabbath", and with the introduction of Sunday shopping and new work patterns in parts of our country, the issues raised in today's scriptures have contemporary relevance for disciples. This is especially the case because the pace of modern life leaves followers of Jesus stressed out much of the time.

There are two controversies about the Sabbath in the Markan collection of five controversies (2.1–3.6). The first features the disciples of Jesus who, going through grainfields on the Sabbath, "made their way … [and] began to pluck heads of grain". The second depicts Jesus present in a synagogue and choosing to heal a man with "a withered hand" on the Sabbath.

The upshot of the two confrontations on Sabbath observance (and possibly the other controversies) is the start of a conspiracy by some Pharisees and Herodians against Jesus (3.6).

The Pharisees pointed out to Jesus the illegal behaviour of his disciples: "Look, why are they doing what is not lawful on the Sabbath?"

Among Jews, the Essenes of Qumran had a strict view of Sabbath observance, forbidding even assistance to birthing animals or ones fallen into a pit or cistern, and similar reactions to a human being (cf. Matthew 12.11 and Luke 13.15-16, where the latter issue is discussed).

The Pharisees, with the rabbis later on, were not so rigorous. Still, they were concerned about spelling out what was and was not permitted on the Sabbath. Reaping on the Sabbath was one of 39 proscribed activities. Only life-threatening situations or dire personal needs superseded the Sabbath law.

Jesus' reply is such a radical reorientation of perspective ("the Sabbath was made for man, and not man for the Sabbath") that his concluding assertion ("so the Son of Man is lord even of the Sabbath") seems to tone it down.

Jesus draws attention to the fact that the Sabbath is part of creation and therefore must be taken seriously. But priorities must be kept in view. The Sabbath was created to benefit humanity, not vice versa.

This finding of a proper place for the Sabbath, rather than reading the text in such a way that people were free to dispense with the Sabbath without qualification, seems the proper understanding of Jesus' answer.

But before coming to his conclusions, Jesus cited a scriptural precedent that justified his disciples. When doing so, Jesus seems to have gotten his Bible history wrong, saying that "Abiathar" was high priest when David entered the house of God, and that David ate "the showbread, which it is not lawful for any but the priests to eat, and ... gave some to his companions". The biblical text of First Samuel (21.1, 2, 8) tells us that Ahimelech, Abiathar's father, was the priest involved.

However, the real issue was the comparison Jesus made between himself and David in providing for his companions. What David could do for his men, Jesus can all the more do – since he is the Davidic messiah – for his disciples. The name of the priest at the time becomes of little consequence.

Healing normally involved some work (preparation of bandages, etc.), so it was not permitted on the Sabbath. Only imminent danger of death created an exception.

As in the earlier case, the issue is one of priorities: is it legal on the Sabbath to do good rather than harm, to save life rather than kill? If doing good involves setting aside scribal interpretation, Jesus does not flinch. The ruling must go. Jesus heals the man's hand and begins his journey to Calvary.

First Sunday of Lent

Beginning Lent's Journey with the New Adam

* Genesis 9.8-15
* Psalm 25
* 1 Peter 3.18-22
* Mark 1.12-15

ARCHBISHOP TERRENCE PRENDERGAST

The word "Lent" comes from the Old English *lencten* and refers to the lengthening of the days as springtime approaches. In this association, the renewal of the earth and of Christian life in baptism are linked.

The Second Vatican Council's decree on the renewal of the Sacred Liturgy stressed two characteristics of Lent: the recalling of one's baptism or preparation for it, and penance. By means of these, "the Church prepares the faithful for the celebration of Easter, while they hear God's word more frequently and devote more time to prayer" (no. 109).

The gospels for the first two Sundays of Lent always feature Our Lord's temptations and his transfiguration, reminding Christians of the struggle against sin – individual and social – for which penance is done, as well as of the glory of Christ that awaits them in overcoming temptation and sin.

The better-known accounts of Jesus' temptation are those found in the Gospels of Matthew and Luke. In these two accounts, a hungry Jesus is urged by the devil to turn stones into bread, to cast himself from the pinnacle of the Temple so that God may send angels to rescue him, and to bow down and worship Satan in exchange for all the kingdoms of the world (cf. Matthew 4.1-11; Luke 4.1-13). All of these temptations Jesus refused, as he parried verbally with Satan and rebutted his subtle suggestions by citing scriptural warrants.

By contrast, Mark's account of Jesus' testing is utterly spare: "He was in the wilderness forty days, tempted by Satan; and he was with the wild beasts; and the angels waited on him". Underlying this tradition is a contrast between Adam and Christ: the disobedience of Adam contrasted with the obedience of Jesus.

Adam yielded to the tempter, leading to hostility with creation and to physical hardships. In overcoming the tempter's traps, Jesus restored harmony to creation and lived on the nourishment provided by God's ministering angels. Thus, there is a new creation, an idea Paul applies to each believer's baptism into Christ's risen life (cf. 2 Corinthians 5.17).

Jesus is the "Second Adam", the obedient servant of God. By example, Jesus teaches disciples to overcome the temptations of life and to serve God through their lives in this world.

The 40-day period of Jesus' testing was instigated by the Holy Spirit, who "drove" him into the wilderness. Believers have linked this time with the 40 years of Israel's wandering in the desert and with the fasts of 40 days conducted by Moses on Sinai (Exodus 34.28) and by Elijah on the way to Horeb (1 Kings 19.8). Curiously, Mark makes no mention of Jesus' fast.

From the role of an accuser of human beings before God (Job 1–2), the Satan came to symbolize God's foremost opponent, ever threatening to break down the rapport between God and human beings. The conflict with Satan's reign and with other areas of conflict and division that marked Jesus' whole ministry (disease, sin, hardness of heart) begins here in earnest.

Mark noted that Jesus was with the wild beasts and that angels ministered to him throughout his temptation. Commentators have observed that humanity living peaceably with the animals was a theme found in the creation accounts (Genesis 1.28; 2.19-20). It was a reality that God's people hoped would be restored in the era of salvation, the new creation.

Jewish writings from Jesus' time and earlier mentioned that angels had fed Adam and Eve in Paradise. Thus, while Adam succumbed to temptation, Jesus – the "New Adam" – under the Spirit's guidance inaugurates a renewed creation in harmony with God.

Jesus' declaration that the time is fulfilled and that people ought to repent points to the new era in which one relates to God by faith ("believe in the good news"). This is the culmination of the covenant God made with Noah, his descendants, and all the living creatures who came out of the ark.

Such harmony of the various elements of creation with each other and with God – symbolized by the rainbow – speaks powerfully to an age such as ours that is anxious about the devastation done to the earth by overconsumption and disregard for the planet.

The First Letter of Peter links the waters of Christian baptism with the renewal of the world through the cleansing power of the flood. Both prepared a people fit for God's covenant of peace.

Second Sunday of Lent

Christ's Glory on the Mountain

* Genesis 22.1-2, 9-13, 15-18
* Psalm 116
* Romans 8.31b-35, 37
* Mark 9.2-10

What to make of the mystery of the Transfiguration remains one of the puzzles of New Testament study. Some see in it features of the resurrection appearances, which are absent in Mark, if the gospel originally ended at 16.8. In resurrection narratives, however, an angel or Jesus generally gives specific individuals a commission to proclaim the resurrection.

In the Transfiguration, by contrast, Jesus commands a time-limited silence: "he ordered them to tell no one about what they had seen, until after the Son of Man had risen from the dead".

The link made with the passion by the words of Jesus is also voiced in the Preface of today's Mass. The celebrant praises God by recalling that Jesus, who had already prepared the disciples for his approaching death, "to show … that the Passion leads to the glory of the Resurrection".

Though the Lectionary omits it, the opening verse observed that the Transfiguration took place "six days" after Jesus began to teach his followers that he would suffer, die and rise. Immediately after this prophecy, Jesus went on to declare that any who wanted to be disciples had to take up their cross and follow him (Mark 8.31-38).

The voice of God from the cloud that overshadowed Jesus and his heavenly visitors affirmed the importance of Jesus' sayings about discipleship, not only by affirming "This is my Son, the beloved", but also by commanding the privileged apostles Peter, James and John to "listen to him!".

These had also been chosen to witness Jesus' raising of Jairus' daughter (Mark 5.37) and would be present at Jesus' agonized prayer in Gethsemane (14.33-41), as were (along with Andrew) recipients of Jesus' apocalyptic discourse (13.3-37).

Peter, James and John regularly gave evidence that they failed to grasp what Jesus was about or how they had to live in keeping with his teaching. On the mountain, this failure to grasp the moment was shown by Peter's words: "Rabbi, it is good for us to be here; let us make three tents, one for you, one for Moses, and one for Elijah". Mark comments, "Peter did not know what to say, for they were terrified".

Still, in this case as elsewhere, Jesus patiently taught his disciples (Mark 9.9-10). He later noted that one day they would be guided by the Holy Spirit, to live in accord with his teaching and to suffer themselves for the sake of the gospel (13.9-11). One might conclude that the ongoing failures of Jesus' disciples were themselves experiences of the cross from which Jesus constantly rescued them, giving them hope.

Moses and Elijah were biblical figures that Jews believed to be alive in God's presence. Because Moses' burial place could not be found (cf. Deuteronomy 34.5-8) and Elijah was taken up to heaven in a chariot (2 Kings 2.1-11), some Jewish traditions held that they had escaped death and were living with God.

In the Transfiguration, however, stress is laid on the paradox of the cross – indeed, on the necessity of Jesus' suffering and death. The latter is presented as the only way for him to enter into the divine glory that, for a brief moment, burst forth onto his bodily features and clothing ("he was transfigured before them, and his clothes became dazzling white, such as no one on earth could bleach them").

The paradoxical way in which God deals with his beloved children is also seen in the text from Genesis. There, on another mountain (in Moriah), God tested Abraham to see whether he would be willing to sacrifice the fruit of divine promise, his beloved son

Isaac. In the drama, God saw that Abraham reverenced him and possessed a disposition totally submissive to the divine will (for the Angel says, "I know that you fear God, since you have not withheld your son, your only son from me").

Origen, an early Christian scholar and theologian, saw in Paul's letter to the Romans that what had not been exacted of Abraham, God offered to humanity out of love. God "did not withhold his own Son, but gave him up for all of us".

Therefore, Paul concluded, "will [God] not with [Jesus] also give us everything else?" The understood answer is "yes". As a consequence, nothing can separate the justified Christian from God's love manifest in Jesus.

Third Sunday of Lent

Words of Everlasting Life

* Exodus 20.1-17 or 1-3, 7-8, 12-17
* Psalm 19
* 1 Corinthians 1.18, 22-25
* John 2.13-25

Reviving Ophelia narrates the challenges facing adolescent girls in a media-driven culture that promotes shallow values. The author cites research suggesting the parenting that can help children pass through the dangers of the teen years to maturity as adults. "Parents who are high in control and high in acceptance (strict but loving parents) have teenagers who are independent, socially responsible and confident. According to this research, the ideal family is one in which the message children receive from parents is: 'We love you, but you must do as we say',"

Whether or not the Ten Commandments are seen as the gift of a strict and loving God to help believers grow into maturity, these words from God are recognized as holding a unique place in Israelite and Christian life. Their special character derives from the fact they are reckoned as God's words, written by the finger of God on stone tablets (cf. Exodus 24.12). Thus, they are and have been regarded throughout history as an extraordinary form of God's revelation. Daily recitation of the Decalogue became a hallmark of certain forms of Jewish life.

By linking the new life of grace inaugurated by Christ with the Ten Commandments as a summary of the obligations inspired by divine charity, St. Augustine contributed to the widespread use of the Decalogue in Church life.

The exterior law of the Ten Commandments thus became interiorized, as Jesus himself had deepened the commandments against killing and adultery by proscribing anger and adulterous desires (Matthew 5.21-28). In his teaching, St. Thomas Aquinas regarded the Decalogue as a summary of the Natural Law.

The catechisms authored by Martin Luther and the Council of Trent both privileged the Ten Commandments in structuring a Christian's moral life. The *Catechism of the Catholic Church* pairs the Beatitudes with the Ten Commandments – along with the Apostles' Creed, the Seven Sacraments and the Our Father – into a contemporary compendium of the faith.

The Ten Commandments are a form of apodictic law: that is, they impose a command directly on a person. They oblige one to perform or refrain from performing some action that is judged harmful.

While these laws are found exceptionally in the ancient Near East, they are characteristic of Israelite life. Using second person singular formulations in the original Hebrew, they contain a measure of intimacy, for in them God speaks directly to the individual believer ("You shall not steal").

The opening commandment centres on God's deeds on Israel's behalf ("I am the Lord your God, who brought you out of the land ... of slavery") and the consequent obligation believers have to worship God alone ("you shall have no other gods before me. You shall not make for yourself an idol"). Then each person is called to sanctify God's name. In Exodus, the command to observe a weekly rest finds its motivation in God's repose following the creation of the world;

in Deuteronomy 5.15, however, the sabbath rest commemorates God's rescue of the Israelites from slavery.

In biblical religion, respect for God is inseparable from respect for one's brother or sister. So, after an instruction concerning one's relationship with God, the Decalogue deals with one's attitude towards others. The command to "honour" one's parents has a promised attached: "so that your days may be long in the land that the Lord your God is giving you".

Next, there are three commandments that tersely forbid murder, adultery and theft. Then, the final three commandments – all of which mention the "neighbour" – spell out implications from the earlier ones: a person may not connive to deprive another of his or her reputation, spouse or any possession that is rightfully theirs.

The Ten Commandments do not embody all that God demands of a believer, but they lay the groundwork for right relations with God and others. In his radical reinterpretation of God's will, Jesus summarized the law and the prophets as demanding that one first love God and "your neighbour as yourself" (Matthew 22.39).

Jesus' righteous anger to fulfill God's purpose led him to "cleanse" the Temple, an act that led irrevocably to his death and resurrection ("Zeal for your house will consume me").

As St. Paul says, "God's foolishness is wiser than human wisdom, and God's weakness is stronger than human strength". The psalm refrain puts it another way: "Lord, you have the words of eternal life".

Fourth Sunday of Lent

John 3.16: "God So Loved the World ..."

* 2 Chronicles 36.14-17a, 19-23
* Psalm 137
* Ephesians 2.4-10
* John 3.14-21

In the Fourth Gospel, the role of Jesus as an evangelizer of people is most clearly seen through his conversations with Nicodemus (3.1-21) and the Samaritan woman (4.1-42). Jesus encountered the woman at the well at midday when no one was around. Gradually, however, the whole village came to hear of Jesus through the woman's testimony. Good news spreads!

The Pharisee Nicodemus came to Jesus secretly at night, suggesting the darkness of unbelief. The ambiguous status of Nicodemus' faith reached its resolution only after Jesus had been crucified. At that point, he and Joseph of Arimathea declared their adherence to Jesus by coming forward to ask Pilate for the body of Jesus for burial (cf. John 7.50-52; 19.38-42).

In meeting a man and a woman – representatives not only of Jews and Gentiles but of all humanity – Jesus led them to greater insight and perception by the use of irony. When Jesus, after asking the Samaritan woman for water, spoke to her of "living" water, she understood him to mean "running" water (as opposed to water from a cistern). But Jesus meant "life-giving" water such as only the Holy Spirit can give the believer from within.

Jesus spoke to Nicodemus about the need to be born "again/from above" (a play on words only possible with the Greek word *anothen*). Nicodemus thought of the impossibility of entering his mother's womb a second time. But Jesus referred to a rebirth that the Spirit makes possible.

A similar play on the Greek word *pneuma*, which means both "wind" and "spirit" (a double meaning possible also in Hebrew), mystified Nicodemus. "The wind [spirit] blows where it chooses", Jesus said, "and you hear the sound of it, but you do not know where it comes from or where it goes. So it is with everyone who is born of the Spirit" (John 3.8).

The third word with a double meaning used in Jesus' interaction with Nicodemus appears in the Greek word *hypsoo*, which means both "to lift up" and "to exalt" (possible also in Hebrew). "Just as Moses lifted up the serpent in the wilderness, so must the Son of Man be lifted up [exalted]" on the cross. The crucifixion is also the moment of Jesus' glorification.

The purpose of Jesus' crucifixion/exaltation was to invite belief from all of those who would see Jesus exposed on the cross. Yet God would save the world thereby.

Indeed, God's purpose is not that the world "perish" but that all come to "have eternal life". "Eternal life" does not mean the endless prolongation of human existence, but rather the joy of dwelling in God's presence forever.

In John's Gospel, such a sharing in eternal life does not get put off until some unknown future (the individual's death or the end of the world). Rather, it begins here and now, as soon as the individual begins to believe in Jesus as the one sent into the world to bring sinners to their rightful status as children of God.

Generally, God is said to "send" his Son into the world to accomplish the world's salvation. But John 3.16 – a text held up for the world's television cameras at concerts and sporting events – describes God's "giving" of Jesus for the sake of the world's salvation: "God so loved the world that he gave his only-begotten Son, so that everyone who believes in him may not perish but may have eternal life".

God's love and God's will are in accord. What began in the Incarnation – the Word of God becoming flesh in the person of Jesus – reached its culmination in his death on the cross and exaltation as the risen Lord.

The letter to the Ephesians sizes up the same reality in slightly different words: "by grace you have been saved through faith, and this is not your own doing; it is the gift of God".

The Book of Chronicles sombrely illustrates how the world and even God's people can wander far from faith, falling into sin ("All the leading priests and the people were exceedingly unfaithful").

But God's purposes cannot be thwarted. Even Cyrus of Persia may be divinely mandated to rebuild God's Temple and thereby help assure the renewal of God's people. Salvation history testifies that God "is rich in mercy"!

Fifth Sunday of Lent

God the Father Glorifies Jesus

* Jeremiah 31.31-34
* Psalm 51
* Hebrews 5.7-9
* John 12.20-33

God's prophets spoke of a new era uniting God and the chosen people under several images. Hosea foretold a new and eternal marriage that would overcome past infidelities on the part of God's bride, Israel (2.18-23). Likewise, Jeremiah predicted the renewal of God's love through "a new covenant" that would be everlasting.

As Lent draws to a close this weekend and next (Passion [Palm] Sunday), the gospel narratives put disciples in touch with the saving mysteries that offer hope and new life: not only to Israel, but also for all the peoples of the world.

Christians hold that Jeremiah's famous prophecy – by which God would place his laws within the human person and inscribe them on human hearts – was realized through Christ's passion, death and resurrection.

This is the central theological conviction of the New Testament, and is found expressed in several texts, notably 2 Corinthians 3.1–5.21 and Hebrews 8.6–9.15.

This new covenant of the heart – with its outcome that people will have no need for others to teach them – is an underlying presupposition of the accounts of the Last Supper, particularly narratives telling the institution of the Eucharist, the new covenant. These appear in the Synoptic Gospels (Matthew 26.20-29; Mark 14.17-25; Luke 22.14-23) and in Paul's First Letter to the Corinthians (11.23-32).

However, the evangelist John does not tell his readers of the establishment of Holy Communion at Jesus' last meal with his apostles.

ARCHBISHOP TERRENCE PRENDERGAST

Instead, in the Fourth Gospel, Jesus gives an extensive discourse on the Bread of Life during his Galilean ministry (6.25-59).

In a similar way, Christians who look for Jesus' prayer in the Garden will find no explicit reference to it in John's Gospel. Still, an attentive reading of today's gospel shows traces of Gethsemane wrapped in Johannine phrases.

For when his death approached, Jesus' soul experienced profound turmoil ("Now my soul is troubled"), as when he confronted the death of his friend Lazarus at the entrance to the tomb (John 11.33-35) and as he would recoil in horror at Judas' betrayal (13.21).

The first chapters of the Fourth Gospel (1–11) emphasized that Jesus' hour had not yet come. But now it has come. The prayer of Jesus, "Father, save me from this hour", expresses a human outlook when faced with death.

But then Jesus asserts that to give himself in death for the salvation of the world is the reason he has come to this hour. So he prays, "Father, glorify your name". (In the Synoptic account of the prayer in Gethsemane, Jesus prays both "Abba, Father, for you all things are possible; remove this cup from me" and a phrase of acceptance and submission: "yet, not what I want, but what you want" [Mark 14.36]).

Then a voice from heaven is heard (though some think it is a clap of thunder – a biblical signal of revelation from God – or an angel speaking), "I have glorified it, and I will glorify it again." In this way, God indicates how pleasing is the teaching and life of his Son.

Jesus had been instructing his followers in the paradoxical logic of eternal life: a grain of wheat must die in the ground to bear fruit, and those who love their life lose it, while those who hate their life (= love their lives less) in this world keep it for eternal life. Service of others, too, is to be the emblem of the disciple of Jesus.

In John's account, Jesus notes that the voice from God came not to benefit him but for his hearers' sake, stressing that his exaltation (his being "lifted up from the earth") would lead all people to be drawn to him in faith.

Whereas the Synoptic Gospels speak of Jesus' death and resurrection, the Fourth Gospel telescopes both events under the image of his being lifted up (all three passion predictions in John use this terminology – cf. John 3.14; 8.28; 12.32). Jesus' being "lifted up" also means the overthrow of Satan's rule: "now is the judgment of this world; now the ruler of this world will be driven out".

The passage from Hebrews may be a variant tradition concerning the prayer of Jesus in Gethsemane. It assures the Christian that Jesus' prayer was heard and that, because of his obedience, Jesus has become "the source of eternal salvation for all who obey him."

Palm Sunday of the Lord's Passion

The Peaceful King Remains with His Church

* Mark 11.1-10 or John 12.12-16
* Isaiah 50.4-7
* Psalm 22
* Philippians 2.6-11
* Mark 14.1–15.47

Some years ago, the media reported the discovery of several coins minted in Galilee around the year 24 AD. Bearing the image of the emperor Tiberius Caesar, they had been overstruck with a palm branch across the ruler's face. The claim of Roman rule was being undermined by a symbol of Jewish resistance.

Two centuries earlier, at the rededication of the Temple, captured from the Syrian ruler Antiochus IV by Judas Maccabbeus and his brothers, people had brought palm branches to the Jerusalem sanctuary. From that Maccabbean period onward, the palm branch gradually evolved into a representation of Jewish nationalism.

In the Fourth Gospel's account of Jesus' triumphal entry into Jerusalem, the evangelist John tells his readers that people brought palm branches to welcome him. John then noted that Jesus had responded to this gesture by riding an ass into the Holy City.

In contrast with the nationalist vision of Jesus' kingship, the evangelist, by means of a combination of texts drawn from the prophets Zechariah and Zephaniah ("Do not be afraid, daughter of Zion. Look, your king is coming, sitting on a donkey's colt!"), offered another.

Instead of riding a war horse or appearing in a military chariot, Jesus entered Jerusalem simply, as a king who offered peace with God rather than a worldly manifesto. On Palm Sunday, Christians commemorating Jesus' entry into the Holy City and the events of his passion are challenged to make their own his vision of right relations with God and the people of our world.

The truth of Jesus' kingship would become visible only at the crucifixion, in the self-emptying love of one who became a suffering servant (Isaiah) and did not "regard equality with God as something to be exploited" (Philippians).

A central aspect of the passion narrative is the final meal Jesus shared with his disciples before his death. The Synoptic Gospel accounts depict it as a Passover meal and the origin of the sacrificial meal that Christians now know as the Eucharist (a word that means "thanksgiving").

A simple comparison of the versions of Jesus' words in instituting the Eucharist shows a range of theological reflection that gives different emphases to Jesus' deeds (the taking, blessing and breaking of bread before giving it to the disciples) and his words. What the gospels preserve is not a literal transcript of what Jesus said, but the core of what he did and said.

This is why, in the Mass, the Church does not slavishly follow one or another version of his words. The words of institution we use today are conflated from several gospel accounts of Jesus' expressed intention to remain with the Church through a sacramental presence in consecrated bread and wine.

Mark's account of Jesus' words over the bread and cup are spare. "Take, this is my Body" stresses the sharing action, as does the fact that Jesus said the words over the cup after "all of them drank from it".

A comparison with Matthew's version shows that his account has paralleled the words of Jesus over the bread and the cup, expanded

Jesus' instructions ("Take, eat; ... Drink from it, all of you" [Matthew 26.26-27]) and included the interpretation of the purpose of Jesus' shedding of "my blood of the covenant, which is poured out for many". The shedding of his blood was "for the forgiveness of sins" (Matthew 26.28).

The account of the Lord's Supper in Matthew and Mark, possibly reflecting a liturgical tradition in the Palestinian Church, interpreted the gift of Jesus' body and blood in the Eucharist as the renewal of the covenant made on Mount Sinai (cf. Exodus 24.3-8).

The accounts handed on by Luke and Paul (1 Corinthians 11.23-27), drawing on the liturgical tradition of the Hellenistic Church, observed in Holy Communion the fulfillment of the "new covenant" foretold in Jeremiah 31.31-34. Only this tradition articulated Jesus' command "Do this in remembrance of me" (Luke 22.19; 1 Corinthians 11.24), though it is presupposed by Matthew and Mark.

New Testament thought on the Eucharist is completed by John's Gospel, which has no reference to the institution of the Eucharist at the Last Supper. Instead, the Fourth Gospel offers a lengthy discourse by Jesus in which he reveals that his flesh is the Bread of Life given for the salvation of the world (6.35-58).

The Resurrection of the Lord: Easter Sunday

The Crucified Lord Jesus Is Risen

* Acts 10.34a, 37-43
* Psalm 118
* Colossians 3.1-4 or 1 Corinthians 5.6b-8
* Mark 16.1-8 or John 20.1-18 or John 20.1-9

En route to the Mount of Olives after the Last Supper, Jesus declared to the disciples that soon they would all abandon him. "You will all become deserters" (Mark 14.27). Peter denied this, "And all of them said the same" (v. 31). None of the disciples, however, attended to the second part of Jesus' prophecy, "But after I am raised up, I will go before you to Galilee" (14.28).

An echo of these verses is found in the gospel reading of the Easter Vigil that may be proclaimed, as well, at the Eucharist on Easter morning: "Go, tell his disciples and Peter that he is going ahead of you to Galilee; there you will see him, just as he told you" (Mark 16.7).

What follows is rather puzzling. Mark says that the faithful women who went to anoint Jesus' body "fled from the tomb, for terror and amazement had seized them; and they said nothing to anyone, for they were afraid". If this is how Mark's Gospel originally ended – namely, without one or more resurrection appearances – it leaves readers puzzled about how the gospel message of Jesus' resurrection became known.

Yet, since readers know that Jesus rose on the third day, that the apostles did proclaim the gospel and some were martyred for the faith, readers must understand that the rest of the promise came to pass and Jesus did reunite his followers in Galilee.

As Peter put it in the reading from Acts, "God raised [Jesus] on the third day and allowed him to appear, not to all the people but to us who were chosen by God as witnesses, and who ate and drank with him after he rose from the dead".

Perhaps the open-ended conclusion to Mark's Gospel should be seen as an invitation to readers to believe the message of the resurrection. As they contemplate in their imagination the disciples' healing encounter with Jesus and his commissioning of them, Christians today are invited by Christ to put into action in their lives their belief in a Lord who is simultaneously the crucified ("you are looking for Jesus of Nazareth, who was crucified") and risen Lord ("He has been raised; he is not here").

In the words of the Letter to the Colossians, Christians are to see themselves as "raised with Christ"; their minds are henceforth set on "things that are above, where Christ is seated at the right hand of God".

Mary Magdalene, Simon Peter and the "Beloved Disciple" all appear in the Fourth Gospel's account of the first Easter morn. In fact, we notice a progression in faith, even if we are left with a sense that there is more to come, a characteristic of the gospels during the Great Fifty Days of Easter.

Mary reported the discovery (by herself and the other women?) of the empty tomb to Peter and "the other disciple, the one whom Jesus loved", saying, "They have taken the Lord out of the tomb, and we do not know where they have laid him".

After running to the tomb and reaching it first, the Beloved Disciple hesitated before entering. In keeping with his headstrong personality, Peter entered immediately and remained wondering at "the linen wrappings lying there" and the [face] cloth "rolled up in a place by itself". Unlike Lazarus, who had to be helped with his linen wrappings (cf. John 11.44), Jesus simply had left the trappings of death behind at his resurrection.

The Beloved Disciple "saw and believed" that Jesus had triumphed over death and the ruler of this world (cf. John 12.31; 14.30; 16.33). The rest would come that evening when Jesus would breathe the Holy Spirit upon the apostles (20.19-23).

Staying behind, Mary received personal knowledge of her risen Lord ("Mary!" ... "Rabbouni!"). As indicated in the Good Shepherd discourse, Jesus knows his own and they know him (John 10.14). Told not to cling to him, because his glorification was not yet complete, Mary received the commission that remains her glory as "apostle to the apostles".

Jesus charged her, "Go to my brothers and say to them, 'I am ascending to my Father and your Father, to my God and your God'". The evangelist tells us that, unlike the frightened women of Mark's Gospel, Mary did as Jesus told her.

Second Sunday of Easter

"Great Grace Was upon Them All"

* Acts 4.32-35
* Psalm 118
* 1 John 5.1-6
* John 20.19-31

Central to the scriptural readings in the Great Fifty Days of Easter are the selections from the Acts of the Apostles. From time to time, after narrating key incidents in the life of the fledgling Church, Luke offered a generalizing statement of what early Christian life was like.

Thus, once he had given an account of the events of Pentecost (Acts 2.1-40), the evangelist related that those baptized "devoted themselves to the Apostles' teaching and fellowship, to the breaking of bread and the prayers" (Acts 2.42).

One community characteristic was their sharing of goods. "All who believed were together and had all things in common; they would sell their possessions and goods and distribute the proceeds to all, as any had need" (2.44-45).

This ideal life nourished the Christians, who spent "much time together in the temple", "broke bread in various houses" and ate "their food with glad and generous hearts, praising God and having the goodwill of all the people" (2.46-47). The fruit of this zealous life was that God daily added to the number of those being saved.

Following the arrest, flogging and release of Peter and John for their preaching of the resurrection of Jesus (3.1–4.31), a second summary of the life of the Jerusalem faith community is presented (4.32-35). Again, unity and the sharing of goods are highlighted ("no one claimed private ownership of any possessions, but everything they owned was held in common").

Thus, the Deuteronomic ideal that there be no poor person in the land (cf. Deuteronomy 15.4) found fulfillment among the followers of Jesus. That "there was not a needy person among them" resulted from disciples selling their possessions and laying them at the feet of the apostles.

Luke's depiction of the harmonious life of the early Christians is meant to edify subsequent generations. And it has! Despite the idealized portrait of the Church, however, we must realize that, then as now, there were different views about how people should handle their possessions.

This point is implicit in the contrasting stories of Barnabas, who sold his land and gave the proceeds to the apostles (4.36-37), and of Ananias and Sapphira, who, though generous to the poor, tried to deceive God and the Church with a false offering (5.1-11).

Luke nowhere suggested that all believers had to dispose of their capital assets, and it is clear that not all did. Each person had to respond to the gospel message as he or she was moved by the Holy Spirit. It is this openness to the Spirit, with resulting joy and mutual support, that gives evidence that God's blessing abided with the Church ("and great grace was upon them all").

The early Church modelled not only how to live ("the whole group of those who believed were of one heart and soul"), but also how to preach ("with great power the Apostles gave their testimony to the resurrection of the Lord Jesus").

Today's gospel reveals that the power to proclaim Christ – who in his risen state still bears the tokens of his sufferings for the salvation of the world ("he showed them his hands and his side") – derives from the Holy Spirit. Jesus confided his own Spirit-driven power to forgive sins, won by his "lifting up" on the cross, when he breathed onto the apostles ("Receive the Holy Spirit"). In the words of the First Letter of John, "the Spirit is the one that testifies, for the Spirit is the truth".

Jesus led the disciples to faith by honouring their need for evidence. While Thomas alone has received the epithet "doubting", Jesus simply gave the one "called the Twin" (of the reader?) what he had earlier given the other ten apostles. As he had shown the ten his wounds, now

Jesus invited Thomas to touch his hand and side and to cease being an unbeliever, becoming a believer instead. Thomas responded with the most complete confession of faith found in the Fourth Gospel: "My Lord and my God!"

Jesus then addressed later generations of Christians, those who would come to know him through the Church's proclamation. He promised that belief would not be limited to those who had seen him, as Thomas and the others had. Rather, "Blessed are those who have not seen and yet have come to believe".

Third Sunday of Easter

"Disbelieving Joy"

* Acts 3.13-15, 17-19
* Psalm 4
* 1 John 2.1-5
* Luke 24.35-48

The risen Jesus' appearance to the Eleven apostles on Easter night draws to our awareness thorny issues about understanding the resurrection narratives. First of all, we note both the discontinuity and continuity between the glorified Jesus and the one the disciples knew before Calvary.

When Jesus appeared in their midst, the apostles thought he was a ghost, so different was his aspect. Then Jesus showed them his hands and feet (allusions to the crucifying nails). He declared that no ghost possessed flesh and bones or ate fish. In other words, he was still the Jesus they had known.

Analysis of the resurrection stories shows that Jesus did not "return to life" in the way Jairus' daughter (Mark 5.35-43), Lazarus (John 11.1-44) or the widow of Nain's son (Luke 7.11-17) had done. Rather, Christians believe that the glorified body of Jesus has entered upon a whole new sphere of life – eternal or everlasting life.

Luke regularly observes that the apostles' disbelief was actually a consequence of sheer joy on their part ("in their joy they were disbelieving"). News of the resurrection appeared to them just too good to be true!

As in other resurrection appearances, Jesus commissioned the disciples to go to others with a summons to repentance. This proclamation is directed "to all nations".

"Beginning from Jerusalem", forgiveness of sins is to be offered to all who repent. Luke shows that the disciples were charged to do this after Jesus interpreted for them all the Scriptures that spoke of him (cf. Luke 24.6-7; 26-27; 44-46).

Proclaiming the forgiveness of sins has always been closely associated with the message of Christ's resurrection. The First Letter of John follows this pattern, but also deals with an issue that intruded upon the Church in the latter part of the first century — how does a disciple continue to be true to the message of Jesus when, after conversion, he or she sins.

Affectionately referring to his fellow Christians as "my little children", the evangelist reminds them that "Jesus Christ the righteous" remains as the Christian's advocate with the Father when the Christian sins.

The image of Jesus here, similar to that depicted in the Letter to the Hebrews (4.14-16), found a place at Mass in the penitential formula "Lord Jesus, you intercede for us with your Father. Lord, have mercy." Henceforth, the forgiven disciple's life consists in walking as Jesus did and obeying his commandments.

Today's responsorial psalm belongs to Night Prayer following Sunday's First Vespers. This points to the Church's conviction that this psalm fittingly refers to Christ's resurrection. Originally a psalm of lament by an individual in Israel, the psalm is now seen as an apt reflection of Christ's passion and resurrection. For Christ is the true holy one, the just one, the only-begotten Son whom the Father loved. Jesus is the one who truly did "lie down and sleep in peace".

In Christian writings, death was referred to as "sleep" (cf. Mark 5.39), even if some versions, like the NRSV, translate the Greek word "sleep" by "died" (cf. Thessalonians 4.13-14). One of the Christian words for resurrection was *anastasis*, the same Greek word used for the act of "rising from sleep". In this sense, the words of the psalmist found their fulfillment in Christ's resurrection. Furthermore, these words will find their counterpart in the coming resurrection of Christ's faithful.

The reading from Acts is an excerpt from the sermon Peter delivered after curing the cripple who sat begging at the Beautiful Gate of the Temple (Acts 3.12-26). Commentators see in the initial chapters of Acts the core structure of the Spirit-filled proclamation that marked the early Church.

After an address to the audience (Acts 3.12), a common pattern in these sermons sees them begin with an Old Testament reference (3.13a), a Christological affirmation (3.13b-15), a 'proof' from Scripture (3.18), and a call to repentance (3.19) that focuses the sermon on the specific needs of the assembled throng (3.17).

In this instance, Luke shows Peter articulating the idea that ignorance underlies some sins ("I know that you acted in ignorance, as did also your rulers"). It is the same sentiment Jesus had expressed during the passion ("Father, forgive them; for they do not know what they are doing" [Luke 23.24]). Ignorance of sin, however, does not preclude a call to repent, an invitation to turn towards the new life God now offers through the risen Jesus.

Fourth Sunday of Easter

Jesus, Shepherd of the Sheep

* Acts 4.7-12
* Psalm 118
* 1 John 3.1-2
* John 10.11-18

The fourth Sunday of Easter – also known as Good Shepherd Sunday – regularly features prayer for priestly vocations. The long address in which Jesus describes himself as the "good shepherd" (John 10.1-21) includes a prior assertion: "Very truly, I tell you, I am the gate for the sheep" (10.7).

Whoever would seek access to God's people as shepherd, then, needs authority from Jesus to do so. Priest-shepherds are called to make their own the selfless dispositions of Jesus, not those of "the hired hand" who runs away in time of danger "because a hired hand does not care for the sheep".

Jesus' speech mentions shepherds, sheep, gatekeepers, hired hands, thieves and bandits, offering a glimpse into rural Palestinian life. The evangelist notes that, in his teaching, Jesus used a "figure of speech" (10.6). This is not the same as a parable – such as the labourers in the vineyard (Matthew 20.1-16) or the Good Samaritan (Luke 10.30-37) – imaginative stories that expand on a metaphor and end with a surprising twist, prompting listeners to reflect on their lives.

Instead, the "figure of speech" is a story of normal everyday life. As Jesus pointed out on various occasions, it is sick people who normally go to the doctor (Mark 2.17), and people do not generally fast at wedding celebrations (Mark 2.18-20) as they would after a death in the family.

So, in the normal course of events, a real shepherd enters the sheepfold in the ordinary way (not coming over the fence) and the gatekeeper recognizes him. Even the sheep know his voice. If a stranger were to try and lead them, the sheep would flee, fearful of the unfamiliar voice (John 10.1-5).

Jesus' contrasting of himself with other religious leaders takes up a theme that goes back to Ezekiel. Through the prophet, God denounced Israel's pseudo-shepherds and pledged to assume the role of Israel's Shepherd (34.1-31).

Jesus received his mission as Good Shepherd from the Father, thereby justifying his claim to be Shepherd of Israel even if people refused to believe him. Not just the shepherd, then, but the sheep, as

ARCHBISHOP TERRENCE PRENDERGAST

well, are undergoing judgment. The issue is whether people hearken to Jesus' voice or not.

Jesus closed the first part of his discourse by declaring he was both the gate leading to salvation ("I am the gate. Whoever enters by me will be saved, and will come in and go out and find pasture") as well as the "Coming One", a variant title of his messiahship ("I came that they may have life, and have it abundantly").

In the second half of Jesus' teaching, what distinguishes the good shepherd from the hireling is that he "lays down his life for the sheep". As Jesus continued to speak, his figure of speech turned into self-revelation ("I am the good shepherd ..."). Though metaphors are employed, the address is all about Jesus and his followers ("I know my own and my own know me, just as the Father knows me and I know the Father").

When Jesus went on to speak about "laying down his life", the issue was no longer that of fighting wolves that were threatening the flock, but of his dying on the cross to bring all people to salvation.

This included the Gentiles to be brought into the one flock by Jesus' disciples ("I have other sheep that do not belong to this fold. I must bring them also, and they will listen to my voice").

Jesus closed his dramatic teaching by declaring the voluntary nature of his death and resurrection ("No one takes [my life] from me, but I lay it down of my own accord ... to take it up again"). This unselfish gift of himself proved that Jesus was fully obedient to the Father, even unto death ("I have received this command from my Father").

Peter's Pentecost speech from the Acts of the Apostles used another metaphor to describe Jesus' resurrection: "the stone that was rejected by you, the builders ... has become the cornerstone".

The consequence of this divine intervention is that now "there is salvation in no one else" but Jesus.

The First Letter of John concludes that Jesus' saving deed made his disciples "children of God" who will grow more and more into his likeness ("when he is revealed, we will be like him").

Fifth Sunday of Easter

"I Am the True Vine"

* Acts 9.26-31
* Psalm 22
* 1 John 3.18-24
* John 15.1-8

The words Jesus speaks in today's gospel are a continuation of his farewell discourse at the Last Supper. It is part of an extended expression of Jesus' legacy to his disciples (John 13.12–17.26).

Its focus evokes ancient biblical images: the vine, vine grower and viniculture practices such as pruning, breaking off dead branches for burning, and harvesting others that produce abundant fruit (John 15.1-17).

For example, a sacred poem depicted God's planting of a vine and its flourishing growth ("You brought a vine out of Egypt ... and planted it") as the culmination of the Exodus event (cf. Psalm 80.7-11).

Also, Isaiah described God crooning a love song to Israel using vineyard imagery (5.1-7); so the vineyard and God's people became interchangeable ("For the vineyard of the Lord of hosts is the house of Israel").

In addition, Jesus told several parables in which vineyard activities were prominent (Mark 12.1-12; Matthew 20.1-16; 21.28-32).

As he did with a number of other images (the bread of life, good shepherd, light of the world, resurrection and the life), by means of the I AM formula Jesus personalized the vine motif ("I am the true vine"). He expanded on the basic theme by commenting on the Father's role ("my Father is the vine grower") and, implicitly, of his disciples' part as branches abiding in him ("as the branch cannot bear fruit by itself unless it abides in the vine, neither can you unless you abide in me").

ARCHBISHOP TERRENCE PRENDERGAST

While other I AM sayings in the gospel include invitations to "come" to Jesus and to "believe" in him (cf. John 6.35), the vine saying invites people, instead, to remain united with Jesus ("abide in me as I abide in you"). Being spiritually linked with Jesus, disciples share in an ongoing and life-sustaining fellowship ("because apart from me you can do nothing").

The First Letter of John develops this vision further, arguing that obedience to God's words, given by Jesus, lies at the heart of this spiritual abiding ("Whoever obeys his commandments abides in him, and he abides in them").

For God's commandments are two-fold, consisting as they do in believing in his Son's name and in loving one another. As the Christian lives out these two commands, the Holy Spirit simultaneously effects and manifests a mystical union between the Christian and his or her Lord ("by this we know that he abides in us, by the Spirit that he has given us").

The first reading offers an example of how great a struggle may be involved in the Christian community's recognition and acceptance of the Holy Spirit's transforming power at work in an individual such as Saul of Tarsus. For Luke, the "conversion" of Paul was so important that he narrated it three times (Acts 9.1-31; 22.6-21; 26.1-23), with each telling of the story focusing on different facets of this dramatic episode in the early Church's life.

In each account, Saul persecuted members of the church and came to learn, through his Damascus Road experience, that Jesus identified with those suffering at his hands. As Saul lay groping on the ground, blinded by his encounter with the Risen Christ, he asked, "Who are you, Lord?" The reply he received was "I am Jesus whom you are persecuting". Once reoriented and converted to faith in Jesus, Saul attempted to join the Jerusalem community, but met resistance when they could not "believe that he was a disciple".

Barnabas, a disciple renowned in Acts for his openness in various ways to the Holy Spirit's work, became an apologist for Saul, testifying "how in Damascus [Saul] had spoken boldly in the name of the Lord".

Despite his all-encompassing ministry in the Holy City ("Saul went in and out among them in Jerusalem"), he roused the ire of a prominent group of Jewish zealots, the Hellenists, so that his life became at risk. Though forced to leave for Caesarea, where he could embark for his native city of Tarsus, this setback would become the providential first step leading to Saul's great missionary voyages once Barnabas had introduced him to the church at Antioch.

Thus, on every page of Acts, Paul became an eminent exemplar of Jesus' dictum "My Father is glorified by this, that you bear much fruit and become my disciples".

Sixth Sunday of Easter

Sharing the Joy of Friendship with Jesus

* Acts 10.25-26, 34-35, 44-48
* Psalm 98
* 1 John 4.7-10
* John 15.9-17

Today's gospel continues Jesus' exploration of the union between himself, the vine, and his disciples, the branches. Abiding in Jesus and reflecting on his words are defined as abiding in his love. Abiding in Jesus' love is equated with obeying his commandments, just as Jesus remained in his Father's love by keeping the Father's commands.

Modelled on Jesus' obedience to the Father, the Christian's adherence to Jesus' teaching is clearly not that of a servant or slave. Rather, its motivation is the example of love given by Jesus ("abide in my love ... love one another as I have loved you").

There is no greater expression of love than the selfless love Jesus manifested for his disciples. This love, shown in his washing their

ARCHBISHOP TERRENCE PRENDERGAST

feet, would come to perfection on the cross. "No one has greater love than this, to lay down one's life for one's friends".

While the disciples rightly call Jesus Teacher and Lord (cf. John 13.13), Jesus suggests that even masters who love their servants do not share with them their inmost thoughts. This he chooses to do, bestowing on them the title of friends: "I do not call you servants any longer, because the servant does not know what the master is doing; but I have called you friends, because I have made known to you everything that I have heard from my Father".

When disciples obey God by following the teachings and example of Jesus, the result is an interior joy ("I have said these things to you so that my joy may be in you, and that your joy may be complete").

The joy that comes from abiding in friendship with Jesus is the fruit of the indwelling Holy Spirit. This joy – drawn from union with Jesus – is contagious and bears rich fruit in the lives of believers.

Under the guidance of the Holy Spirit, the joy and fruitfulness of intimacy with Jesus occasionally becomes manifest in unexpected ways. This may be noted over and over again in the Acts of the Apostles. And nowhere is this more strikingly so than in the case of the conversion of Cornelius.

As the extent of the early Church's ministry broadened, a significant barrier had to be crossed: bringing the gospel directly to Gentiles. So important was the insight to do so – as illustrated by the story of the conversion of Cornelius and his entourage – that Luke devoted 66 verses to it (Acts 10.1–11.18) and dramatized the story with a set of interlocking visions shared by Peter and Cornelius.

Several aspects of Cornelius' conversion are emphasized in Luke's account. First, the evangelist noted that the early Church resisted either directly evangelizing Gentiles or receiving them into Christian fellowship without associating them with Judaism ("the circumcised believers who had come with Peter were astounded that the gift of the Holy Spirit had been poured out even on the Gentiles").

Secondly, it was God who introduced the Gentiles into the Church and miraculously showed approval of this step ("Then Peter said, 'Can anyone withhold the water for baptizing these people who have received the Holy Spirit just as we have?'").

Thirdly, even though Paul is heralded as the "apostle to the Gentiles", it was Peter who was God's instrument in opening the door to the Gentiles ("So [Peter] ordered them to be baptized in the name of Jesus Christ").

Finally, the Jerusalem Church subsequently recognized that Gentile believers could accept Jesus as the Messiah without becoming Jews because God had so determined ("I truly understand that God shows no partiality, but in every nation anyone who fears him and does what is right is acceptable to him").

This initial conclusion (Acts 11.18) would later be formally ratified at what has become known as the Council of Jerusalem (15.1-29), the first of a series of Church councils that stretches to the Second Vatican Council in our time (1962–65).

The notion of God going ahead and preparing human hearts and the Church to accept conversion or a new perspective has been designated as "prevenient grace" in Christian theology. The First Letter of John underlines this point, observing, "In this is love, not that we loved God but that he loved us and sent his Son to be the atoning sacrifice for our sins".

The Solemnity of the Ascension

The Risen Jesus Empowers His Church

* Acts 1.1-11
* Psalm 47
* Ephesians 4.1-13
* Mark 16.15-20

The conclusion to Mark's Gospel is the source of some controversy because of differences found among early manuscripts. Some of the best manuscripts end at Mark 16.8, which – if it is the original conclusion – implies that the evangelist concluded his gospel message without reporting appearances of the Risen Jesus.

There are grounds for thinking this was deliberate on Mark's part, thereby inviting readers to make an act of faith in the resurrection message. This conviction has led a number of gospel commentators to pass over interpreting verses beyond Mark 16.8.

Other scholars theorize that Mark's original ending has been lost; perhaps the last part of the original codex (manuscript in the form of a book) broke off. Some have suggested that Mark's Gospel seemed deficient when compared with the other gospels, which narrated apparitions by the risen Lord.

Accordingly, early Christian believers made various efforts to resolve what seemed to them to be an unsatisfying ending. One such conclusion, the "short ending", reads, "And all that had been commanded them they [the women] told briefly to those around Peter. And afterwards Jesus himself sent out through them, from east to west, the sacred and imperishable proclamation of eternal salvation".

The canonical or "long ending" of Mark (16.9-20), though regarded by the Church as inspired scripture, is non-Markan in content, style and vocabulary. Consisting mainly of traditions about Easter that are drawn, it would seem, from the other gospels (Mark 16.9-14), the Markan appendix seems to have been designed as a manual of instruction to answer questions about Jesus' resurrection appearances and spell out their theological meaning (16.15-20).

What these various endings illustrate is the way in which the Church continued to see the Easter experience as pivotal. The resurrection and glorification of Jesus (in the ascension) are central to the Church's history and belief; they are at the origin of the Christian community's missionary preaching and service to the world.

Jesus' missionary mandate – "Go into all the world and proclaim the good news to the whole creation" – parallels and re-expresses the Great Commission found in Matthew 28.19 ("Go ... and make disciples of all nations").

Both stress the universality of the mission to the Gentiles. Emphasis is placed on the importance of believing and on baptism as the response to the gospel message ("The one who believes and is baptized will be saved; but the one who does not believe will be condemned").

The promise of charismatic gifts to believers ("by using my name they will cast out demons; they will speak in new tongues; they will pick up snakes in their hands") shows the Church's conviction that such signs are continuing marks of Christian faith. Only the mention of drinking "any deadly thing" without harm is without mention elsewhere in the New Testament, though miraculous escapes are referred to.

The Ascension is described in 16.19 in terms borrowed from Psalm 110.1 ("And sat down at the right hand of God"), a key text in New Testament descriptions of the lordship of Jesus. Unlike the general portrait of the disciples elsewhere in Mark, here the disciples obey Jesus ("they went out and proclaimed the good news everywhere").

In a text reminiscent of the Acts of the Apostles, the closing words show that Christ's Ascension initiated and made possible the Church's missionary proclamation of the gospel. Though in heaven, Christ Jesus is not regarded as distant from his Church ("the Lord worked with them and confirmed the message by the signs that accompanied it").

Luke tells the story of Jesus' Ascension twice: briefly at the conclusion of his gospel narrative (Luke 24.50-53) and in a more developed form at the beginning of Acts (1.1-11). This helps show that the visible ministry of Jesus – brought to conclusion with the Ascension – and the life of the Church are a continuous whole. Luke also stresses the Holy Spirit's role in propelling the Church into the whole world as witnesses to Jesus ("you will be my witnesses to the ends of the earth").

The question posed by the apostles ("Lord, is this the time when you will restore the kingdom to Israel?") and Christ's reply ("It is not for you to know the times or periods that the Father has set by his own authority") establish an eschatological framework for world

ARCHBISHOP TERRENCE PRENDERGAST

history. Jesus has been exalted to heaven and will return; between these two points, the Church lives its life determined by them.

Seventh Sunday of Easter[1]

The Prayer of Jesus and His Church

* Acts 1.15-17, 20ac-26
* Psalm 103
* 1 John 4.11-16
* John 17.11b-19

Today's liturgy takes place during the first *novena* (nine days) of prayer in the Church's history. This period of prayer was prescribed by Jesus when he left the disciples at the Ascension.

This first "Novena to the Holy Spirit", then, was observed by the early Church as it awaited the outpouring of spiritual blessings from on high at Pentecost.

Given this context, the theme of this Sunday reflects various forms of prayer – first *intercessory* prayer, that the Church discern how to deal with betrayal within the Twelve; then *hymnic* prayer, praise for God's blessings in the responsorial psalm; and finally an extract from the *High Priestly Prayer of Jesus* (John 17.1-26), wherein he asks the heavenly Father that his disciples be "sanctified".

The fruit of the sanctification for which Jesus prayed enables the disciples to live, amidst the circumstances of their world, in love for one another (second reading).

The church's intercessory prayer in the Acts of the Apostles seeks enlightenment from God about the divine will regarding a replacement for Judas Iscariot, so that the number of the "Twelve Apostles" might be complete.

---

1 For use in countries and ecclesiastical provinces where the Ascension is celebrated on Thursday.

The first reading omits a brief description of the traitor's death (1.18-19) and a partial verse from Psalm 69.25 (1.20b), which foretold the desolation of the homestead Judas bought with the money he received for handing Jesus over (Luke 22.47-54).

Peter assembled a body of about 120 men, the minimum number needed to establish a community with its own council. In Jewish terms, the "brothers" (the first time this term is used of the disciples is in Peter's address) were sufficient to constitute a new community.

Now the focus falls on the divine through interpreting the Scriptures; by establishing criteria for an apostle based on the will of Jesus (choosing "one of the men who accompanied us during all the time that the Lord Jesus went in and out among us, beginning from the baptism of John until the day he was taken up from us – one of these must become a witness with us to his resurrection"); through prayer and the casting of lots.

While intercessory prayer is often used in the Scriptures to make known individual intentions, here such prayer is directed to a communal purpose – to benefit the community – and to discover what God wants. Frequently, allusion is made in this passage to the "divine necessity" – what God has ordained – in the past or present tense (Greek past tense *edei*, "it was necessary" [1.16] or present tense *dei*, "it is necessary" [1.21; cf. also Luke 22.37; 24.26, 44; Acts 3.21; 17.3]).

Lot casting was a traditional biblical way of determining God's will (cf. Joshua 19.1-40; Jonah 1.7-8). After the names of Joseph Barsabbas – "Justus" in Latin – and Matthias were put forth and possibly written on stones, the name that emerged was that of Matthias.

So God's will is discerned by a community of faith whose values include Scripture (1.20), a close relationship with Our Lord (1.21-22) and petitionary prayer (1.24-25). The community then, in obedience to the determination God had made in answer to their intercessory prayer, added Matthias to the Eleven Apostles.

The hymnic prayer of Psalm 103 speaks of "all [God's] benefits", including casting sins "as far as the east is from the west". Taken within the context of the first reading, this affirms the healing that the choice of Matthias represents for the Christian community, renewed and restored after the betrayal by Judas.

Jesus' high priestly prayer asks for his disciples the protection of the heavenly Father ("protect them in your name", i.e. by your power), even as he foresaw the defection of "the one destined to be lost, so that the Scripture might be fulfilled". This allusion to what Scripture foresaw underscores that the loss of Judas cannot void the security of Jesus' care, but belongs to the divine plan.

Jesus addresses God as "Holy Father" to underline the desire that his disciples share in God's holiness by their being sanctified through his prayer. The purpose of this request is that the unity of the faith community may always mirror the unity that Jesus shares with his Father.

The life of the community after Jesus' hour (the paschal mystery) is entrusted to God by Jesus. This protective care of Jesus for his disciples will ensure that, though the disciples are in the world, they will not be "of the world" – that is, they will not be guided by a disposition hostile to God.

Pentecost Sunday

"The Rush of a Violent Wind" and "Tongues of Fire"

* Acts 2.1-11
* Psalm 104
* Galatians 5.16-25
* John 15.26-27; 16.12-15

Easter, the new Passover, and Pentecost – the Jewish celebration 50 days later – are the hinges of the Church's liturgical year. The Greek Old Testament twice used "Pentecost" to designate the "feast of weeks", the second of Israel's three great annual pilgrimage celebrations (the third is the feast of "booths" in the fall).

In the Hellenistic era, the covenant God made with Noah (Genesis 9.8-17) was renewed, but after the destruction of the Temple Pentecost was associated with God's bestowal of the Torah on Sinai. For Luke, Pentecost fulfills Jesus' promise to his followers that they would be empowered once they had received the Holy Spirit from on high (Acts 1.5, 8; cf. Luke 24.49).

The evangelist does not tell his readers where the early community was gathered when the Holy Spirit came, only that "they were all together in one place". Tradition suggests the group of believers numbering about 120 persons – the minimum number in Jewish law to establish a new community – met in "the room upstairs" (Acts 1.13). Whatever its precise location, there they gathered around the apostles, "with certain women including Mary the mother of Jesus, as well as his brothers", and devoted themselves to prayer.

Powerful symbols describe the Spirit's coming: there was "a sound like the rush of a violent wind"; also "Divided tongues, as of fire, appeared among them, and a tongue rested on each of them". These were the outward signs of the invisible reality, that "All of them were filled with the Holy Spirit".

The subsequent external manifestation of the indwelling Spirit was that these all "began to speak in other languages, as the Spirit gave them ability".

Elsewhere in Scripture, the "Spirit" is likened to the "wind" (cf. John 3.8). In fact, in Greek, *pneuma* has both meanings. The noise made by the violent wind of the Holy Spirit was so palpable that its sound seemed to have "filled the entire house where they were sitting".

In the past, God's presence at Sinai had been accompanied by a loud sound (cf. Exodus 19.16-19), while a turbulent wind had been associated with the theophany to Elijah (1 Kings 19.11-12) as well as Elijah's ascent to God in the flaming chariot (2 Kings 2.11).

God had been revealed to Moses in the flaming bush (Exodus 3.2), and the image of a fire was often featured in moments of divine presence. John the Baptist foretold that God's coming in judgment would be manifest in a divine, cleansing fire (cf. Luke 3.16). Luke's

ARCHBISHOP TERRENCE PRENDERGAST

description of the divided flames says that a tongue came to rest on each person. It is interesting to note that in Jewish tradition, fire occasionally was said to rest on the heads of rabbis when they studied or disputed about God's law.

The ancient world valued highly ecstatic speech because it was thought to derive from direct possession by the deity. Paul's discussion of the phenomenon of *glossolalia* or "speaking in tongues" (cf. 1 Corinthians 10–12) suggests that ecstatic, babbling speech was known at Corinth.

Luke stresses not the ecstatic but the communicative feature of this religious experience ("each one heard them speaking in their own languages"). One commentator tries to resolve the two types of speech by suggesting that the hearers thought they heard and recognized words of praise to God in their own dialects ("in our own languages we hear them speaking about God's deeds of power").

The sequence in the list of nations present at the first Christian Pentecost ("Parthians, Medes, Elamites ...") has long fascinated interpreters, but no one has yet been able to give a satisfactory explanation for its origin (a list of nations where Jews resided?) or the order in which regions are mentioned.

The catalogue of nations begins in the east and moves westward, from Persia and Iran towards modern Iraq, with Judea – where Jerusalem is located – suddenly appearing in the midst of the pattern. Next, areas of Asia Minor are mentioned, then Egypt and the region west of it; finally comes Rome, capital of the Empire, where Acts will terminate.

"Jews and converts" suggests that mix of God's people and Gentiles who would be fashioned by "the Spirit of truth" into the mystery called the Church.

In Galatians, Paul shows that the Spirit helps believers overcome the "desires of the flesh" to produce "the fruit of the Spirit".

The Most Holy Trinity

God's Nearness: "I Am with You Always"

* Deuteronomy 4.32-34, 39-40
* Psalm 33
* Romans 8.14-17
* Matthew 28.16-20

The Book of Deuteronomy – which means "second law" – addressed the religious, social and political crises of Israel after the twelve tribes had settled in the Promised Land. Within this prophetically inspired document, Moses rehearsed the people's sacred history from Mount Horeb (Deuteronomy's name for Mount Sinai) through the transition into Canaan, exhorting God's chosen collectively and individually (the text oscillates between the second person plural and singular in the Hebrew) to obey God's Torah.

Loyalty to God had become compromised both by worship of Canaanite gods in the cities and by fertility rites conducted on the high places scattered throughout the country.

Socially, a breakdown in family solidarity had occurred as a result of the shift from an agricultural barter system of exchange to a money economy. The gap between rich and poor was widening, and institutions founded to protect the poor were in need of revitalization.

Politically, the judicial system had become corrupt through bribery; consequently, it failed those most in need of justice and protection.

The Deuteronomic reform envisioned a new society based on renewed dedication to God and divine teaching. God's decrees were to penetrate all aspects of Israelite life. Henceforth, justice for all would be the prevailing rule, and the poor would be protected from the greed of the rich.

ARCHBISHOP TERRENCE PRENDERGAST

In presenting this new vision, great rhetorical skill was marshalled in an attempt to convince believers to accept the far-reaching reforms proposed ("Ask now about former ages, long before your own ...; ask from one end of heaven to the other, 'Has anything so great as this ever happened or has its like ever been heard of?'")

In harking back to the Exodus and its culmination at the foot of God's mountain, the sacred author pointed out the uniqueness of Israel's experience: "has any people ever heard the voice of a god speaking out of a fire, as you have heard, and lived?" Fidelity to this encounter with the unique Lord God revealed to Israel ("there is no other"), would assure well-being and long life with God "in the land that the Lord your God is giving you for all time".

For Christians, the only God of the universe has become manifest in a totally new way in the person of Christ, the risen Lord. His divinity led the disciples to adore him, even if a degree of resistance persisted among them ("When [the eleven disciples] saw him, they worshipped him; but some doubted").

This glorified and majestic Jesus declared that God had given him sole authority over all the inhabitants of the earth ("All authority in heaven and on earth has been given to me. Go therefore and make disciples of all nations ... teaching them to obey everything that I have commanded you").

Baptism in the name of the Trinity would be the sign that people assented to God's revelation in Jesus ("baptizing them in the name of the Father and of the Son and of the Holy Spirit").

Only Matthew records Jesus' command to baptize, but the practice of the early Church supports its historical nature (cf. Acts 2.38; 8.12, 38; 9.18; etc.) Early accounts of the Church's baptismal practice sometimes refer to the sacrament as having been administered "in the name of Jesus Christ" (Acts 2.38; 10.48) or "in the name of the Lord Jesus" (Acts 8.16; 19.5). Clearly, there was a variety of baptismal terminology used by the early Church before the Trinitarian formula became normative.

Baptized "into the name" reflects a Hebrew or Aramaic thought structure and implies that disciples undergoing baptism are henceforth "fundamentally determined by" or "ruled by" the Father, Son and Holy Spirit. Though the Persons of the Trinity are mentioned, use of the singular "name" in their regard points to the unity of the three.

In his letter to the Romans, Paul struggled to express the changed relationship that Christ's death and resurrection effected in each believer's status before God. The outpouring of the Holy Spirit into human hearts enables each disciple to call out to God just as Jesus did, "Abba! Father!"

Sharing in the life of the Trinity now will one day lead to inheriting the kingdom with Jesus ("heirs of God and joint heirs with Christ").

The Most Holy Body and Blood of Christ

The Renewal of God's Covenant in Jesus' Blood

* Exodus 24.3-8
* Psalm 116
* Hebrews 9.11-15
* Mark 14.12-16, 22-26

During Holy Week this year, the entire passion narrative was read twice: from Mark's Gospel on Palm Sunday of the Lord's Passion and from John's Gospel on Good Friday. When the entire narrative is read, the rich theological themes of the passion come all at once; it can prove difficult to absorb more than one or two of them.

Today's solemn commemoration of *Corpus Christi* (the Body [and Blood] of Christ) allows for a deepened appreciation of the key mystery of Catholic belief. That is, in the celebration of Holy Communion, the bread and wine are changed into the Body and Blood of Christ, serving as heavenly food for the Christian to live out the teaching of Jesus on his or her journey to God's kingdom.

There are four accounts of the institution of the Eucharist: one in each of the Synoptic Gospels (Matthew 26.26-30; Mark 14.22-26; Luke 22.14-20) and a fourth in Paul's First Letter to the Corinthians (11.23-27).

Close examination of the four versions shows that Luke's and Paul's accounts are similar, perhaps reflecting liturgical traditions of the Church at Antioch, while Mark's and Matthew's resemble each other, possibly paralleling a formula used in Jerusalem.

Mark often stresses Jesus' ability to predict the future: his sufferings and subsequent glory, as well as the failure of his disciples and their reconstitution in Galilee (14.27-28). So today's gospel opens with Jesus arranging for the celebration of a Passover meal. He asked two of the disciples (Luke identified them as Peter and John [22.8]) to go into Jerusalem, where they would meet a man carrying a water jar – an unusual sight, as this was women's work.

The Benedictine archaeologist Bargil Pixner has suggested that this person was someone associated with the Essenes, and that Jesus observed Passover according to the Qumran calendar. Since the Essene observance of Passover that year would have been a couple of days ahead of that celebrated by the rest of the Jews, this might explain the Synoptic view that the Last Supper was a Passover meal, whereas John maintains that it happened the day before Passover.

In his account of the Last Supper, John's focus is on Jesus' humility in washing his disciples' feet; Johannine teaching on the Eucharist is found in the Bread of Life discourse, which will be presented this year in the Sunday readings of August.

When the stranger showed them the large upstairs room, they prepared the Passover there. Surrounding the eucharistic words are Jesus' predictions of his coming betrayal by Judas (14.17-21) and the falling away of Peter and the rest (14.27-31). Even though his disciples fall short, Jesus promises that God's purposes will be realized in Jesus' resurrection and formation of the nascent church in Galilee (16.7).

Jesus ended his words over the bread and the cup by asserting an unshakeable conviction that, though betrayed, his act of abstaining from wine would culminate in celebration and he would commemorate a victory in the coming kingdom: "I will never again drink the fruit of the vine until that day when I drink it new in the kingdom of God" (14.25).

The words Jesus pronounced over the bread ("Take; this is my Body") are sparse by comparison with the Paul/Luke tradition ("that is for you"/"which is given for you"), but the symbolism of his breaking the bread points to the coming gift of his life on the cross.

Jesus' words over the cup ("This is my Blood of the covenant, which is poured out for many") echo the text from Exodus, the first reading of today's liturgy. Just as Moses had sprinkled the blood of sacrifice, half on the altar representing God and half on the people God had chosen to symbolize their union, Jesus united himself with his weak and struggling disciples by a bond that can never be broken.

The "blood of the covenant" created solidarity between two parties involved. In biblical thought, this bond is based on the understanding that blood is the distinctive element that makes life possible.

At Sinai, Israel began a new life of obedience, signified by the sacrificial meal offered up and acceptance of the "book of the covenant" read out by Moses and the "Blood of the covenant" acted out in a marvellous liturgy. So, too, does the Church in the Lord's Supper.

Tenth Sunday in Ordinary Time

Jesus Is the One Who Sets Free

* Genesis 3.8-15
* Psalm 130
* 2 Corinthians 4.13–5.1
* Mark 3.20-35

With Mark as our guide, the next two weeks afford an exploration of Jesus as the teller of parables (Mark 4.26-34) and the one who stills both wind and waves (4.35-41).

This week we meet the one who is stronger than Satan and thus is able to overthrow the reign of the devil and his minions. For Jesus is mighty enough to despoil Satan's house.

Jesus declared that forgiveness was available from God for every sin and blasphemy – with a single exception ("whoever blasphemes against the Holy Spirit"). By the power of his declarations about how things are between God and humanity, Jesus set people free from those bonds that keep people from heeding the call of the kingdom – even such good bonds as link a person to his or her family.

After Jesus had been carrying on his ministry for some time, people began drawing conclusions about what they saw. Two groups are singled out for raising objections. First – and somewhat surprisingly, we might think – Jesus' family expressed concern for his behaviour. When throngs made it impossible for Jesus to carry on a normal way of life (he was unable even to eat), his kin tried to restrain Jesus. Mark said things had come to such a point that "people were saying 'He has gone out of his mind'".

Then Mark's readers learned that some scribes, who had come down to Galilee from Jerusalem, asserted that Jesus' power to exorcise unclean spirits was itself demonic. For they were maintaining, "He has Beelzebul, and by the ruler of demons he casts out demons".

Now one of the literary features Mark favours is something that has been dubbed the "sandwich technique". Within a particular story (for example, the clash between Jesus and his family in Mark 3.21, 31-35) the evangelist often inserts a second story (the charge of demonic possession, 3.22-30). Other examples of Mark's "sandwich" or framing technique may be detected in other passages as well (6.7-13, 30-32; 9.37, 41; 11.12-14, 20-26; 14.1-2, 10-11; 14.54, 66-72).

As the gospel narrative continues, Mark regularly resolves the second issue, and then returns to the first. In this way, each story within the frame or sandwich comments on the other one, and the whole structure appears more striking. Thus, the charges of mental illness and demonic possession are associated in a way that helps today's reader see how out of the ordinary Jesus' ministry struck his contemporaries as being.

One may also conclude that family ties, if they prevent one from becoming a disciple of Jesus and joining his true family ("whoever does the will of God is my brother and sister and mother"), can approach the demonic.

Which brings us to the "sin against the Holy Spirit" that has caused wonder through the ages. From the context, it would seem that the "eternal sin" – beyond forgiveness – consists in attributing the effects of the Holy Spirit, working through Jesus, to demonic sources. In other words, Jesus declared that sins can be forgiven as long as people do not cut themselves off from the source of forgiveness, the Holy Spirit.

In healing the paralytic, Jesus, the Son of Man, had already declared that God's forgiveness is offered to everyone (cf. Mark 2.1-12). Jesus' Spirit-guided ministry healed people in both body and spirit. In this way, Jesus invited all to follow him, becoming members of his and God's family by doing the divine will.

Sadly, even today people seem to prefer traditional patterns of personal, family and social life than the radical changes to which Jesus summons them. Yet faith recognizes that it is Jesus' way that leads out of troubled situations and into greater health and spiritual happiness.

In Genesis, we note that sin destroyed the harmony that once existed between the woman and the man made in God's image. Before sin, the couple's nakedness without shame in God's presence symbolized their intact relationship with God.

After sin, the shame and guilt they felt before God represents the rupture in their friendship with God. Christ's resurrection, however, will one day give all believers a new body ("the earthly tent") "eternal in the heavens".

Eleventh Sunday in Ordinary Time

Jesus' Parables Surprise and Challenge

* Ezekiel 17.22-24
* Psalm 92
* 2 Corinthians 5.6-10
* Mark 4.26-34

ast week Jesus used parabolic speech to refute the charge that he was in collusion with Satan: "If a house is divided against itself ... that house will not be able to stand". By asserting that "no one can enter a strong man's house and plunder his property without first tying up the strong man", Jesus claimed power greater than the "ruler of the demons". The time of Jesus' ministry truly meant the overthrow of Satan's realm.

Parables are short stories taken from everyday life that offer a surprising turn or reversal of expectations. The unusual twist in the story provokes reflection, inviting its hearer to make a decision about how he or she might live in light of the truth revealed by the parable.

For, as Paul reminded the Christians of Corinth, "all of us must appear before the judgment seat of Christ, so that each may receive recompense for what he or she has done in the body, whether good or evil".

In chapter 4, Mark draws together several parables to show how Jesus helped his listeners imagine the new reality of God's kingdom (4.1-34). The parable of a farmer sowing seeds that produced extraordinary yields – even a hundredfold (Mark 4.1-20) – appeared in the liturgy last year when Matthew's account was read.

This week we explore a parable unique to Mark's narrative – the seed growing "without his knowing how" (4.26-29) – along with the parable of the mustard seed (4.30-32), which appears in several versions in the Synoptic Gospels, as well as in the apocryphal Gospel of Thomas. Lastly, we see how Mark brings the parable collection to a conclusion with comments on the reason Jesus taught in parables (4.33-34).

One parable said that God's kingdom was like seed planted by a farmer that grew day and night until the harvest came. This parable noted three distinct moments in the dynamic process of the kingdom: sowing, growth and harvest.

This brief similitude moves back and forth between the seed and the farmer. The first part stresses the farmer's action in sowing and the conclusion of his role in harvesting. The central part observes that the seed sprouts and grows on its own, even "without [the farmer] knowing how".

The parable invites people to grasp that God's kingdom germinates, grows and matures without enhancement from visible external causes. The parable challenged those who saw little evidence of God's presence in Jesus' ministry or the Church's early days. The story invited them to believe in a hidden mystery at work in their midst.

The parable says little about the time between seeding and harvest. All the while, however, growth is taking place, and the time of harvest – the consummation of God's reign – must be near. In biblical literature, images of harvest implied notions of judgment. People would be called to account – did they act when they learned that God's kingdom was in their midst and required a response from them?

The mustard seed parable stresses a surprising contrast, between the smallness of the seed and its growth into a plant where birds can nest in its shade. The metaphor seems to be a surprising choice for Jesus' description of God's kingdom. One would have thought that discussion of God's sovereignty over people's lives would have demanded a stress on the kingdom's greatness!

Jesus' use of the mustard seed to illuminate God's kingdom underlined the infinitesimal dimension of God's rule relative to popular expectations in his time. Still, smallness was not the whole story. For the fully grown mustard plant "becomes the greatest of all shrubs".

In contrast with Ezekiel (17.3-4; 31.3-9) and Daniel (4.20-22), who called on tree imagery to represent various kingdoms, Jesus used a bush to represent God's fully developed kingdom. The mustard seed parable tells of a kingdom that, for all its marvellous expansion, remains lowly.

By comparison with worldly kingdoms (great trees), God's kingdom (the mustard bush) does not seem unusually large. But it has branches large enough "that the birds of the air can make nests in its shade".

Ezekiel had spoken of God taking a cedar twig and causing a great tree to sprout from it. In the shade of this tree's branches would "nest winged creatures of every kind". When Jesus spoke of nesting birds, he suggested the inclusive nature of God's kingdom, open to all nations on earth.

ARCHBISHOP TERRENCE PRENDERGAST

Twelfth Sunday in Ordinary Time

Jesus Calms Wind and Waves

* Job 38.1-4, 8-11
* Ps 107
* 2 Corinthians 5.14-17
* Mark 4.35-41

The account of Jesus' stilling of a storm on the Sea of Galilee offers several insights into the struggle by disciples to understand their Lord. The Christian reader may note the serenity of Jesus sleeping on a cushion in time of imminent danger, then gaze in awe at the authority with which he tamed the chaotic power of nature.

With two words meaning "be silent", "be still", Jesus admonished wind and waves, as earlier he had rebuked unclean spirits (Mark 1.23-28; 3.11-12). Faced with the reproach addressed by his followers ("Teacher, do you not care that we are perishing?"), Jesus chided them for their lack of faith ("Why are you afraid? Have you still no faith?")

The reverential fear with which the story closes ("they were filled with great awe and said to one another, 'Who then is this, that even the wind and the sea obey him?'") is meant to evoke a similar wonder today about Jesus' identity. For Jesus is shown – in this miracle over the forces of nature – to manifest a power attributed to God alone in the Old Testament.

As the disciples had done in their plea to Jesus, the people of Israel formerly had "cried to the Lord in their trouble, and he brought them out from their distress; he made the storm be still, and the waves of the sea were hushed" (Psalm 107.28-29).

When finally God answered the righteous sufferer Job "out of the whirlwind", no justification for the problem of suffering was given. Instead, God invited Job to believe that suffering was within the mysterious design of the universe's Creator, who "laid the foundation of the earth". We are told that within God's design for the world there is place for losses, setbacks, storms and disasters.

From the divine soliloquy we learn that it was in God's hands to set limits to the seas, to say, "Thus far shall you come, and no farther, and here shall your proud waves be stopped". With this biblical framework in mind, we see the early Church declaring that Jesus possessed a share of the divine power extending over the forces of nature.

Mark's story of the stilling of the storm on the lake was only the first of several miracles that took place around the sometimes treacherous Sea of Galilee, where sudden gusts of wind can change a simple boat journey into a harrowing adventure.

In the other narratives, Jesus cleansed a demon-possessed man dwelling in caves of the Gentile "country of the Gerasenes" (Mark 5.1-20), healed a woman who suffered from hemorrhages, and brought the twelve-year-old daughter of Jairus back to life (5.21-43). Jesus' charge to the long-suffering woman underlines the key message of the whole unit: "Do not fear, only believe" (Mark 5.36).

Throughout history, artists and preachers have seized on the image of the disciples in the boat with a sleeping Jesus at their side. The storm-tossed boat is an image of the Church universal sailing through the ages. A cross is sometimes used to depict the mast of the boat, for the paschal mystery is at the core of Christian life.

Jesus is present with the Church and concerned for its well-being even when his care is not perceived. Although death lurks close by, Jesus rises up and overcomes even this hostile power called death, to share with his followers the calm of the resurrection.

Paul's Second Letter to the Corinthians dwells repeatedly on the threat of suffering and imminence of death in the apostle's life and, by extension, in that of the Christian believer. When Paul was rescued by Christ from almost certain death, he experienced a foretaste of the victory God would one day give him through the coming resurrection.

Paul said he had once regarded Jesus only "from a human point of view". Now, however, he has experienced the new way of life that faith makes possible. The only way to describe this new reality is by a term such as "a new creation".

ARCHBISHOP TERRENCE PRENDERGAST

"Everything old", Paul declared, "has passed away; see, everything has become new". This changes not only one's perception, but one's behaviour, too, so that disciples "might live no longer for themselves, but for him who died and was raised for them".

Thirteenth Sunday in Ordinary Time

"Do Not Fear, Only Believe"

* Wisdom 1.13-15, 2.23-24
* Psalm 30
* 2 Corinthians 8.7, 9, 13-15
* Mark 5.21-43

Prior to the healing miracles of today's gospel reading, Jesus had been in the country of the Gerasenes on the Gentile side of the Lake. There he exorcised a demon-possessed man who had been living among the tombs and, contrary to his normal practice of invoking secrecy, sent him away to spread throughout the Decapolis, a league of ten Hellenistic cities, the good news of what the Lord in his mercy had done for him (5.1-20).

The paradox of concealment and revelation continues in the healing of a woman who had suffered from hemorrhages for twelve years and the bringing back to life of the twelve-year-old daughter of a synagogue leader named Jairus (5.21-43).

The woman "told him the whole truth" of how she had been healed of her ailment when she had merely touched his cloak. Then Jesus strictly demanded that the parents of the little girl (and his disciples Peter, James and John) not let anyone know how he had restored her to life. This despite the fact that, moments earlier, people had been weeping and wailing loudly at her death.

The story of the healing of Jairus' daughter is told in two parts, with the story of the bleeding woman's cure sandwiched in the middle. This joining of the stories, perhaps effected by Mark rather than what was present in the oral and written traditions he had received, allows the central theme of faith to be doubly articulated at the mid-point.

After the woman told how power issuing from Jesus had healed her, Jesus interpreted what happened in these words: "Daughter, your faith has made you well".

And when news was brought that Jairus' little girl had died and there was no need to 'trouble the teacher any further', Jesus encouraged the leader of the synagogue with the following invitation: "Do not fear, only believe".

The restoration to life of the "little girl" (we hear Jesus using his native Aramaic, calling her "Talitha") embodies the truth taught in the Book of Wisdom that "God did not make death" but merely allowed it through "the devil's envy". Rather, "God created [us] for incorruption, and made [us] in the image of his own eternity" so that one day all diseases would be healed.

The woman's menstrual affliction, besides being a physical discomfort and weakness, rendered her ritually impure and so unable to take part in the normal life of the faith community (cf. Leviticus 15.25-31). After so many years, she might have thought her situation incurable, but she had taken hope from what she had heard about Jesus.

However, the touch of an "unclean" woman would have rendered him ritually unclean, too; hence her decision to be as discreet as possible, touching only the hem of his garment. Her notion about merely touching his garment and the way the miracle gets described ("immediately aware that power had gone forth from him") may strike modern readers as somewhat magical (cf. also Mark 6.56). However, Jesus responded to her limited understanding and gave her not the rebuke she expected but encouragement and the invitation to "go in peace ... healed of your disease".

Paul summed up Jesus' sympathy for human frailty and incomprehension in a paradox expressing the generous act of Our Lord Jesus Christ's incarnation: "though he was rich [in divine status], yet for your sakes he became poor [in entering the human condition], so that by his poverty you might become rich".

Paul continues his reflection on Christ's generous self-giving by inviting his fellow Christians to believe that God's lavishness can spur us on to sharing the abundance of which we have all received. Here is one of the motivating principles for Christian stewardship: the generous giving to others some part of the time, talent and treasure received from a God who pours out blessings on his children.

In urging generosity in support of others, Paul always leaves the individual disciple free to give to the extent that he or she feels moved. No one should be constrained ever to give to charity.

Still, Paul invites the Christian, who strives to reflect Christ Jesus in their way of life, to seek a balance between excess on the one hand and penury on the other. He notes that this principle is enunciated in Scripture (Exodus 16.18): "The one who had much did not have too much, and the one who had little did not have too little".

Fourteenth Sunday in Ordinary Time

Paul's "Thorn in the Flesh"

* Ezekiel 2.3-5
* Psalm 123
* 2 Corinthians 12.7-10
* Mark 6.1-6

Something that has fascinated Christians over the centuries is the meaning of an affliction Paul referred to near the conclusion of his Second Letter to the Corinthians. While speaking of mystical graces accorded him by God ("a person in Christ who fourteen years ago was caught up to the third heaven"), Paul went on to say that to keep him from being too elated, "a thorn was given to me in the flesh, a messenger of Satan to torment me".

Learned commentators have speculated on the nature of Paul's "thorn in the flesh". Identifications of it range from a bodily ailment (epilepsy, migraine, malaria, ophthalmia, a speech impediment) to something mental (bouts of depression, an experience of despair) or even spiritual (a temptation of some kind). Some focus on the term "messenger of Satan" and surmise Paul meant his persecutors or Christians who regarded him as a heretic.

Whatever it was, the thorn in Paul's flesh seems to have begun around the time of his visionary experience and continued up to the time of his writing this letter. Perhaps he needed to be brought down to earth after his being "caught up to the third heaven".

But Paul did not see it that way. So, he three times prayed to be relieved of what humiliated him and seemed to interfere with the effectiveness of his ministry. The answer to Paul's prayer taught him that the same God who had given him the spiritual experience had also given him the thorn.

Paul knew that many Corinthians – like other people in the ancient world and even some people today – expected their religious leaders to have visions and revelations, tokens of God's blessing. With this expectation, the Corinthians probably did not expect visionaries also to be humbled by some sort of affliction, an experience of what we may characterize as the shame of the cross.

Paul received his vision and revelations in the third or highest heaven, sometimes called Paradise. Paul did nothing to bring about such a mystical experience. Rather, it was given him by God. Nor would Paul permit himself to speak boastfully about it. For he had "heard things that are not to be told, that no mortal is permitted to repeat" (2 Corinthians 12.4).

Paul's mystical journey came about entirely by God's grace. Remarkably, the thorn in his flesh occasioned another revelation. In reply to Paul's prayer, "the Lord" – doubtless this refers to Jesus – taught Paul a profound lesson: "My grace is sufficient for you, for power is made perfect in weakness".

Paul could have learned many lessons from suffering. That, when borne patiently, suffering produces strength of character. Or that within oneself one may find inner resources to endure those afflictions that come with life. Instead of these teachings, however, Paul was invited to look beyond himself and see God's power at work in the weakness of his human condition.

ARCHBISHOP TERRENCE PRENDERGAST

Not knowing precisely what Paul's thorn in the flesh was, Christians in every era can identify with Paul's frustration and need of divine assistance as they face their own experience of an unwanted "thorn in the flesh".

Likewise, disciples find themselves invited to make Paul's conclusion their own: "I will boast all the more gladly of my weaknesses, so that the power of Christ may dwell in me". Thus, God's grace enables many in every age to conclude with Paul and proclaim, 'whenever I am weak, then I am strong'.

In a similar vein, the gospel today depicts for us a Jesus who paradoxically is unable to do a "deed of power" in his hometown of Nazareth, "except that he laid his hands on a few sick people and cured them". This came about because Jesus was taken aback "at their unbelief".

Jesus declared that this experience of his had always and everywhere been the lot of the prophet ("A Prophet is not without honour, except in his hometown, and among his own kin, and in his own house").

Ezekiel was addressed by God more than 90 times as "ben adam" (literally, "son of man", which the NRSV regularly translates as "mortal") to underline his frailty and to show that it is divine power that becomes manifest in a prophet's words. Jesus chose the literal rendering "Son of Man" to describe himself as a means to both conceal and reveal his prophetic mission from God.

Fifteenth Sunday in Ordinary Time

Telling About God's Kingdom in Word and Deed

* Amos 7.12-15
* Psalm 85
* Ephesians 1.3-14
* Mark 6.7-13

The introduction to Mark's Gospel (1.1-15) concluded with Jesus heralding the kingdom and inviting people to change the direction of their lives ("Jesus came to Galilee, proclaiming the good news of God, and saying, 'The time is fulfilled, and the kingdom of God has come near; repent, and believe the Good News'" [1.15]).

As the gospel progressed, Jesus took a definitive step by choosing a group of men known as the Twelve for the two-fold purpose of companionship and mission: "And he appointed twelve, whom he also named apostles, to be with him, and to be sent out to proclaim the message, and to have authority to cast out demons" (3.14-15).

Now that the Twelve had been with him for several chapters, had heard his teaching and witnessed the miracles he has performed, in today's gospel reading Jesus sends his disciples out on mission.

Like Jesus, they "went out and proclaimed that all should repent. They cast out many demons, and anointed with oil many who were sick and cured them". In the manner of Jesus they would also be said to teach those they encountered, for after their mission, Mark noted that they reported to Jesus "all that they had done and taught" (6.30).

There are several versions of Jesus' instructions to those he sends out with the charge of preaching the gospel of God (cf. Luke 9.3-6 and 10.2-12; Matthew 10.5-15). Yet in interpreting these instructions for those going on mission today, we must avoid literalism in trying to understand how the Church today should go on mission.

We must acknowledge that in several instances, what is said in one version is the opposite of what is found in another. For example, in Mark's account Jesus told his followers that they may take a staff and wear sandals, whereas in Luke's version the apostles are forbidden to take a staff (9.3) and the 70 sent out in Luke 10.4 are told to "carry no sandals".

We must try to understand what underlies each set of instructions. Because the Twelve had received spiritual empowerment from Jesus, God's protection would be with them. They need not worry about supporting themselves along the way. God who has given them a share in Jesus' authority over unclean spirits will supply their needs.

Though Mark stresses their accomplishments, Jesus warns the Twelve that, like himself, they must expect to be rejected by some.

ARCHBISHOP TERRENCE PRENDERGAST

Though they bring God's peace to those who accept their message, they must be ready – as the prophets were – to warn of God's judgment on those who reject them and move on ("shake off the dust that is on your feet as a testimony against them").

The blessing that opens Ephesians is an overture to the entire writing. In this blessing, the mystery of God's saving plan is depicted in terms of the past (before time or creation existed), the Christian present (including what has been revealed in and by Christ), and the future (a pledge to Christians of inheriting God's redemption): "[God] chose us in Christ before the foundation of the world to be holy and blameless before him in love".

The most visible proof of God's purpose is found in the union between Jews and Gentiles ("we have also obtained an inheritance"; "you also … heard the word of truth, the Gospel of your salvation") that finds expression in the inclusive phrase "our [common] inheritance".

The poetry of Amos is filled with imagery drawn from his shepherd background. This he used to denounce the hollow prosperity of the Israelite kingdom. He was the first to use the phrase the "Day of the Lord" to signify that divine wrath was about to be visited not against Israel's enemies, but against Israel herself for departing from moral uprightness.

The God of creation and history requites all unrighteousness.

Wondrously, the fulfillment of God's design for the world's salvation happens in ordinary ways. In the ministry of prophets like Amos who cried out for social justice. In preaching and the healing ministry of the apostles sent out on mission by Jesus. In the manifold ways in which today's Church carries on the service of Christian faith. That is, by the Church's spiritual ministries and in the Church's proclamation of that justice for God's little ones, which authentic faith demands.

Sixteenth Sunday in Ordinary Time

"Shepherds After My Own Heart"

* Jeremiah 23.1-6
* Psalm 23

* Ephesians 2.13-18
* Mark 6.30-34

"I will give you shepherds after my own heart" (Jeremiah 3.15). In these words from the prophet Jeremiah, God promises his people that he will never leave them without shepherds to gather them together and guide them: "I will set shepherds over them [my sheep] who will care for them, and they shall fear no more, nor be dismayed" (Jeremiah 23.4).

These are the opening words of Pope John Paul II's 1992 Apostolic Exhortation *Pastores Dabo Vobis*. In it the Pope addressed the "formation of priests in the circumstances of the present day".

There the Holy Father expressed the Church's perennial need for shepherds to guide God's flock: "Without priests the Church would not be able to live that fundamental obedience which is at the very heart of her existence and her mission in history, an obedience in response to the command of Christ" to make disciples of all nations, to announce the Gospel and to renew daily the sacrifice of the cross in the Eucharist.

The Pope's pastoral letter to the Church contends that God continually calls forth priests from the people. The challenge in our day is to help those who have been chosen to hear God's summons and to respond generously.

Many young men who have the aptitude for priestly service struggle – like Jeremiah himself did – with feelings of being inadequate to the task they are called to embrace ("Ah, Lord God! Truly I do not know how to speak, for I am only a boy" [1.6]).

But God generously offers them, as he did the prophets, assurance of divine help in facing the life of service to God's people: "Do not say, 'I am only a boy'; for you shall go to all to whom I send you, and you shall speak whatever I command you. Do not be afraid of them, for I am with you to deliver you" (1.7-8).

Regularly, texts from the prophets foretell a dramatic, divine intervention in human history to set right conditions that are not fitting for the chosen people, God's handiwork. In this spirit, Jeremiah

ARCHBISHOP TERRENCE PRENDERGAST

declared that God would dismiss selfish shepherds who had proven themselves unworthy of his flock. God would introduce another, selfless type of pastor.

In place of the inadequate shepherds who would be dismissed, God declared, "I myself will gather the remnant of my flock ... I will raise up shepherds over them who will shepherd them".

The person to implement this change would be a descendant of David's lineage, a king who would rule wisely. He would be known as the incarnation of God's righteousness ("the Lord is our righteousness"). God's holiness would somehow be extended through this mysterious figure to all God's people.

Today's gospel shows the apostles returning from their ministry of teaching and healing. After their mission, Jesus summoned them to "Come away to a deserted place all by yourselves and rest a while".

This gesture shows the profound wisdom of Jesus in desiring that his associates have time to debrief, to reflect on what they had experienced and to give themselves over to relaxation and prayer.

However, the crowd caught sight of Jesus and his disciples' movement, understood where they were heading and flocked to their company. Jesus showed them compassion. And to meet their needs "He began to teach them many things". Mark's description stresses not only the great lack among the people, but also the sufficiency of Jesus' teaching to meet their needs.

What began in Jesus' preaching, teaching and miracles found definitive fulfillment in the paschal mystery – the passion, death and resurrection of Christ.

With sustained use of the terms "reconcile" and "reconciliation", the teaching of Ephesians stresses the effect of God's saving act in Christ's crucifixion, namely a profound change in relationships between God and humanity: from anger, hostility and alienation to love, friendship and intimacy (cf. 2 Corinthians 5.19).

Realizing that there are, in many dioceses, echoes of Mark's description of the people who came to Jesus as being "like sheep without a shepherd", we pray for an increase of worthy candidates for the priesthood.

May they hear and heed God's call to shepherd the flock so that all who belong to Christ Jesus, the Good Shepherd, "shall not fear any longer, or be dismayed, nor shall any be missing".

Seventeenth Sunday in Ordinary Time

Taking the Initiative

* 2 Kings 4.42-44
* Psalm 145
* Ephesians 4.1-6
* John 6.1-15

John the evangelist's account of the multiplication of the loaves has striking affinities with the first Synoptic feeding story (Mark 6.31-44 and parallels): the lonely place, the five loaves and two fishes, the five thousand people present, green or much grass, twelve baskets of leftovers, and Jesus' withdrawal to the mountain.

Emphases unique to John, however, are also numerous: Jesus goes up the mountain at the beginning; the closeness of Passover is indicated; no reason is given for Jesus' feeding the people; the giving out of the bread is attributed to Jesus; and Jesus gives a reason for gathering the fragments ("so that nothing may be lost").

The role of the crowd is also highlighted: they gather because of Jesus' "signs"; they declare Jesus to be "the Prophet"; and the crowd is not dismissed – rather, Jesus slips away because they want to proclaim him their messianic king.

Also, Jesus is the "prophet like me [Moses]" (cf. Deuteronomy 18.15) of the last days (keeping vigil on the mountain), but is greater than Moses. Jesus, the Bread of Life come down from heaven. Is the true Messiah come into the world.

At the centre of John's narrative is Jesus; the disciples slip into the background. Jesus does not perform the feeding miracle to ease the crowd's distress, but to reveal himself in a special way through this feeding.

ARCHBISHOP TERRENCE PRENDERGAST

The disciples are foils for Jesus in the Fourth Gospel. Unlike the Synoptic feeding accounts, the hunger of the crowd is not mentioned. Jesus knows what he is about: awakening in the crowds hunger and thirst for eternal life.

Though the exalted Christology of John's Gospel may cause Jesus to appear distant, through this miracle he appears as devoted to others. Finally, though the crowds – who wanted to make Jesus into a political figure – misunderstood the miracle, Jesus corrected false interpretations about his works.

Echoing the Old Testament lesson, Jesus gave the reason for gathering the fragments: not to avoid wasting food, but to show that Jesus offers a food that does not perish (6.27). More profoundly, Jesus asserted that it was the divine will that he should lose nothing of all that the Father had given him (6.39).

Today's gospel shows several people taking initiative: the crowd, Andrew and a little boy, and Jesus. The crowd's energy seemed boundless; they followed Jesus around Lake Tiberias hoping for a miracle (vv. 1-2), drew near to him on the mountain (v. 5), concluded that he was "the Prophet" who was to come into the world (v. 14), and tried to force him to become their king (v. 15).

There is something slightly misguided in each one of these actions. And yet, they effected an encounter with Jesus that led to an offer of eternal life. Only at the end of John 6 would tragedy ensue: though people accepted the multiplied bread, they refused Jesus' offer of his flesh as real food and his blood as real drink.

In John's Gospel, Andrew is the honest broker who introduces his brother Peter (1.41-42), the Greeks (12.22) and this lad (6.8-9) to Jesus.

Jesus asked a question about feeding the crowd to test Philip, because Jesus already knew what he was going to do. From the outset, then, we see that the initiative belonged to Jesus. And since John had earlier told his readers that Jesus "knew what was within the human person" (2.25), we may presume he foresaw how the crowd would draw wrong conclusions from the miracle.

Despite – or perhaps because of – this misunderstanding, Jesus brought the crowds to that point of decision where they could hear Jesus declare his intention to offer himself as their food, thus revealing that the initiative is always God's. Indeed, God regularly takes the initiative (giving manna in the wilderness [v. 31]; seeing that Jesus would lose nothing [vv. 12, 39]; and ensuring that all who believe would have eternal life [v. 40]).

When we have examined all the initiatives in the gospel today – the crowd's, Andrew's and the young boy's, Jesus' – we discover that underlying them all, the initiative is God the Father's. This is the mystery to be explored in depth on the next several Sundays.

Eighteenth Sunday in Ordinary Time

"I Am the Bread of Life"

* Exodus 16.2-4, 12-15, 31a
* Psalm 78
* Ephesians 4.17, 20-24
* John 6.24-35

A striking episode in the Israelites' wandering in the wilderness after their escape from bondage in Egypt was the story of their feeding on manna, "a fine flaky substance, as fine as frost on the ground" (Exodus 16.1-36).

The Hebrew words *man hu*, which underly the term "manna", literally mean "what [is] it?" Moses offered the people the correct theological interpretation: "it is the bread that the Lord has given you to eat".

On their departure from Elim towards the wilderness of Sinai (Exodus 16.1), Israel faced a crisis of leadership ("the whole congregation of the children of Israel complained against Moses and Aaron"). Specifically, the people questioned their leaders' (and, implicitly, God's) ability to provide them with food, water and other means to support life.

ARCHBISHOP TERRENCE PRENDERGAST

Notable in the wilderness challenge was the way in which memories of Egypt were transformed by hunger and weariness. Egypt had been the place of abuse and oppression, but now was recalled as the place of meat and bread ("we sat by the fleshpots and ate our fill of bread").

God answered the rebellion of his people by supplying them with quails at night and manna in the morning. Though not reflected in the Sunday Mass reading, the spirit of the Israelites was far from adhering to the divine dispositions. People were greedy, taking more than they needed, and some even sought manna on the Sabbath, though God had given each family unit a double share on the Sabbath eve.

The text of Exodus 16 is the crucial background for understanding Jesus' bearing and teaching in every phase of his "Bread of Life" discourse (John 6.25-65). Jesus began his interpretation of the miracle of the loaves and of the crowd's zeal to find him by challenging their motives ("you are looking for me, not because you saw signs, but because you ate your fill of the loaves").

Jesus then contrasted two kinds of food: the perishable and the imperishable ("Do not work for the food that perishes, but for the food that endures for eternal life, which the Son of Man will give you"). With exaggerated concern about the necessities of life comes the personal temptation to want to trust in both the bread from heaven (a free gift from God) and the bread of this earth (which is earned by the sweat of one's brow).

Jesus, in urging disciples to pray for one's daily bread (which can stand for all that sustains – including home, family and relationships), says that seeking to have it both ways simply exacerbates a tendency to anxiety. His gospel teaching plainly builds on the lessons from the journey of Israel in the desert: that God knows what people need and faithfully supplies all that is needed for life.

The crowd – as so often happens in John's Gospel – ironically misunderstood Jesus' words about "working for" imperishable food. For Jesus, the only necessary work is to believe in the one on whom God "has set his seal" of identification and sent into the world ("This is the work of God, that you believe in him whom he has sent").

Jesus said they only had to work at receiving the gift God was offering. Instead, the crowd focused on their own performance of deeds to achieve God's work ("What must we do to perform the works of God?"). Furthermore, the crowd demanded to see an additional sign before believing in Jesus ("What sign are you going to give us then, so that we may see it and believe you? What work are you performing?").

In citing the manna story, Jesus reinterpreted it in several ways. The giver of manna was not Moses but Jesus' Father. The giving of the heavenly food was not past, but continues into the present. By contrast with the earlier manna, the food Jesus spoke about is "true" bread, and it is his hearers, not their ancestors, who are the beneficiaries of God's gift ("it is my Father who gives you the true bread from heaven").

When the crowd asked Jesus for this bread, his startling answer was, "I am the bread of life. Whoever comes to me will never be hungry, and whoever believes in me will never be thirsty". The deep meaning of this truth Jesus will reveal in coming weeks.

Nineteenth Sunday in Ordinary Time

"I Am the Bread that Came Down from Heaven"

* 1 Kings 19.4-8
* Psalm 34
* Ephesians 4.30–5.2
* John 6.41-51

Today's gospel reading continues the Johannine "Bread of Life" discourse in which the central unit of John's sixth chapter (6.26-59) consists of an extended homily by Our Lord on several Old Testament passages: a) "He [God the Father] gave" (verses 26-34); b) "bread from heaven" (verses 35-47); "to eat" (verses 48-59).

ARCHBISHOP TERRENCE PRENDERGAST

Jesus' address in the synagogue of Capernaum is broken up by several interruptions (verses 30-31, 34, 41-43, 52). These serve both to engage the audience's interest and to surface difficulties felt by people in Jesus' time and that of the evangelist.

Today's gospel reading is composed of one such interruption (6.41-43), part of the central section where the bread Jesus gives parallels the wise teaching of biblical works like Proverbs (vv. 44-47), and the beginning of Jesus' description of the gift of himself in sacramental terms (vv. 48-51).

People started to find fault when Jesus claimed, "I am the bread that came down from heaven". So they commented unfavourably on what they thought were his human origins ("Is not this Jesus, the son of Joseph, whose father and mother we know? How can he now say, 'I have come down from heaven'?").

Although John's Gospel does not have a narrative about the infancy of Jesus, nor does it refer to stories about his birth, it seems likely that these remarks make ironic allusion to such traditions. Note, for example, the irony observable in John 7.41-42 for someone who knows of Jesus' birth in Bethlehem: "Surely the Messiah does not come from Galilee, does he? Has not the scripture said that the Messiah is descended from David and comes from Bethlehem, the village where David lived?"

The Fourth Gospel affirms that Jesus is the Son of God (John 1.17) and is convinced that aspects of his earthly family ties hold no role in understanding his identity.

Now Jesus addresses the crowd – who persist in a grumbling, complaining mode – for a second time. Jesus restates the key theological point he made earlier: that God's initiative is everything ("No one can come to me unless the Father who sent me draw them" ... "Everyone who has heard and learned from the Father comes to me").

The prophets, Jesus says, agree on this point, as he quotes a paraphrase of the Septuagint (Greek) version of Isaiah 54.13 ("It is written in the prophets, 'and they shall all be taught by God'").

With the words "Very truly, I tell you", Jesus begins a new unit affirming that belief is the key to obtaining eternal life ("whoever believes has eternal life"). Jesus then declares that he *is* the bread of life, moving from a sapiential interpretation (i.e., that his teaching gives meaning to people's lives) to a sacramental understanding of himself (as nourishment for the hunger of the world): "I am the living bread that came down from heaven. Whoever eats of this bread will live forever; and the bread that I will give for the life of the world is my flesh".

The eucharistic imagery is not yet explicit – it will become so in next weekend's unit, verses 52-58 – but the movement of Jesus' imagery is becoming very clear.

The direction of Jesus' thought has progressed rapidly. First, Jesus is the giver of bread, a new Moses and one who surpasses Elijah's miracle (first reading). Second, Jesus is also the purveyor of the bread of revelatory wisdom, nourishing all who come to him in faith. Finally, Jesus is the origin of the eucharistic gift of eternal life for all who would eat the flesh and drink the blood of the heavenly and glorified Son of Man.

For the author of Ephesians, Christian discipleship has a two-fold dimension. Putting aside ways of life that are incompatible with following Jesus ("bitterness and wrath and anger and wrangling and slander, together with all malice") and embracing those in keeping with it ("be kind to one another, tenderhearted, forgiving one another, as God in Christ has forgiven you").

Christians are called to "be imitators of God ... and live in love, as Christ loved us and gave himself up for us".

Further, yielding to the Spirit in one's life is not a once-for-all happening, but an ongoing challenge: "Do not grieve the Holy Spirit of God, with which you were marked with a seal for the day of redemption".

ARCHBISHOP TERRENCE PRENDERGAST

Twentieth Sunday in Ordinary Time

God's Wisdom Leads to Jesus' Gift of Himself

* Proverbs 9.1-6
* Psalm 34
* Ephesians 5.15-20
* John 6.51-58

Wisdom – the sapiential tradition found in the Bible and in the ancient world generally – taught that there were basically two ways, two attitudes towards life and, hence, two personifications (the wise person and the fool).

The house built by Wisdom may be understood as the school in which Wisdom reigns. Wisdom was present at the world's construction (Proverbs 8.27-30) and was delighted to live within it (8.31). Wisdom's "house" referred to the natural world, with its seven pillars representing "perfection". Wisdom may be acquired by observing nature and all that the processes of life have to offer.

Bread and wine, in Old Testament times, represented the staples of life and so these items were used in cultic actions at God's Temple. By feasting on Wisdom's offerings, newcomers to the educational process would be encouraged to put aside worldly enjoyment out of love for and delight in learning. This implied leaving behind former companions and other ways of living ("Lay aside immaturity, and live, and walk in the way of insight").

A key biblical truth was that the "fear of the Lord" was the beginning of wisdom, a truth articulated by the psalmist: "Come, O children, listen to me; I will teach you the fear of the Lord. Which of you desires life, and covets many days to enjoy good?"

Most often in biblical texts, fearing God equates with reverence for, trust in and dependence on God. The fear of God means constantly seeking God's will and then taking refuge in God and his designs: "My soul makes its boast in the Lord; let the humble hear and be glad".

In its broad sweep, Psalm 34 tells of God's life-giving activity and urges people to experience it for themselves ("Taste and see that the Lord is good ...").

The wisdom of the psalmist contradicts the values of today's consumerist culture, which assails believers at every turn.

Media advertising emphasizes the value of possessions and status. Scripture, by contrast, stresses that dwelling in a trusting relationship with God brings joy and fulfillment in all circumstances.

God refreshes the spiritually crushed but, for all that, does not quash the forces that create injustice. God's care mends broken hearts, yet paradoxically does not prevent them from being broken. This anticipates the paschal mystery, where the Lord's resurrection gives meaning to suffering, and where his broken body and poured out blood – given in the Eucharist – offer life to those who believe.

The first part of Jesus' "Bread of Life" discourse invited disciples to come to him for life: "I am the bread of life. Whoever comes to me will never be hungry, and whoever believes in me will never be thirsty". These words may be understood as a parallel to Wisdom's invitation: coming to Jesus and feeding on him is to embrace his teaching, to live his way of life.

In the last of Jesus' address, however, his words take on a particular focus, that of communing with him, feeding on his body and blood in the Eucharist. Jesus' earlier invitation to "eat this bread" now becomes to "eat the flesh of the Son of Man and drink his blood".

The terms "flesh" and "blood" in Hebrew refer to the bodily nature of human existence, underlining the truth that the heavenly Son of Man truly became incarnate: that is, took on human existence. But for every Christian these words contain unmistakeable echoes of the eucharistic sacrifice.

Eating the flesh and drinking the blood of Christ in communion now become the condition for receiving the life he offers ("unless you eat the flesh of the Son of Man and drink his blood, you have no life in you").

Jesus' gift of eternal life, which will come to its fullness in the resurrection from the dead ("I will raise them up on the last day"), takes effect when the believing disciple receives Jesus' gift of himself in the Eucharist ("whoever eats my flesh and drinks my blood has eternal life").

In his teaching, Jesus opens to his fragile followers the possibility of sharing in God's own life. As Father Raymond Brown put it in his magisterial commentary, "while the Synoptic Gospels record the institution of the Eucharist, it is John who explains what the Eucharist does for the Christian".

Twenty-first Sunday in Ordinary Time

Covenantal Relationships

* Joshua 24.1-2a, 15-17, 18b
* Psalm 34
* Ephesians 4.32–5.2, 21-32
* John 6.53, 60-69

One conviction dominates the Book of Joshua – that God had destined Israel to become a covenant people in a special land. A "covenant" established a relationship of trust and commitment joining two partners (in this case, God and Israel), with each assuming obligations.

God's recurrent promise of posterity and land to the patriarchs and their families had finally come to pass under Joshua's leadership. In response, the groups forming the people of Israel committed themselves to keeping the Torah precepts given to Moses.

The last chapter of the Book of Joshua features a sacred ceremony at Shechem, during which the Israelite tribes pledged allegiance to God (24.1-28). Most scholars see this account as the first such pledge of loyalty ("we will serve the Lord"); others think it reflects an ongoing – perhaps annual – covenant renewal ritual.

The service began with Joshua telling in God's name all the history they had experienced on the way to the Promised Land (24.3-13). Remarkably, no mention is made in this narrative of the events at Sinai or the wilderness traditions.

In a gesture unparalleled in the Bible, Joshua offered the people a choice – to worship either other gods or the Lord. In the continuation of his speech after the people chose to serve the God who had intervened in their lives (24.19-27), Joshua warned of disasters that would come upon Israel if they proved unfaithful to the covenant they had entered with God – a message that, sadly, later came true.

There is a note of sadness in the gospel when readers learn that some who had been Jesus' disciples stopped following him ("many of his disciples turned back, and no longer went about with him"). Jesus concluded his teaching on the Bread of Life by underlying the people's need to "eat the flesh of the Son of Man and drink his blood". Without feeding on him in the Eucharist, "you have no [eternal] life in you".

When some stated that this was a difficult teaching – hard to accept – Jesus' reply touched on several points. Equally offensive to them would be his being lifted up on the cross and his resurrection, the preludes to his glorification ("what if you were to see the Son of Man ascending to where he was before?").

Jesus noted, as well, that there is a radical cleavage between the worlds of the spirit and the flesh ("the words that I have spoken to you are spirit and life"). Those who do not believe belong to "the flesh", which – in John's Gospel – regularly refers to that feature of human nature that resists or opposes God.

As he does in other gospel traditions, Simon Peter speaks on the disciples' behalf a declaration of faith, that Jesus is the "Holy One of God". When Jesus queried the Twelve whether they also would leave him, Peter voiced covenant trust on behalf of all believers: "Lord, to whom can we go? You have the words of eternal life".

The covenant relation of most Christians is the loving commitment to their marriage partner. Paul's advice to the Ephesians strikes some Christians as outdated, even troubling. Indeed, the exhortations of Paul ("Wives, be subject to your husbands ... Husbands, love your wives") have been used to justify spousal abuse and other familial hurts.

These instructions, however, were a significant development in their day and have the potential to be a blessing today. The First Letter of Peter and the letters to the Ephesians and Colossians develop their culture's fashion for "household codes" (instructions for spouses, children and parents, slaves and masters) by adding to them Christian motives ("as you are to the Lord" ... "just as Christ loved the Church and gave himself up for her").

Some people in the first century looked down on the body and devalued sexuality. But the spousal union is beautiful, Paul says, and each partner should love the other's body as one's own ("no one ever hates his own body, but he nourishes and tenderly cares for it, just as Christ does for the Church").

It is a message that challenges those today who would cheapen sexuality, marriage and lifelong fidelity. As does Paul's governing principle for both husbands and wives: "be subject to one another out of reverence for Christ".

Twenty-second Sunday in Ordinary Time

"Welcoming the Implanted Word"

* Deuteronomy 4.1-2, 6-8
* Psalm 15
* James 1.17-18, 21-22, 27
* Mark 7.1-8, 14-15, 21-23

For people who worship God regularly, Psalm 15 offers a thoughtful catechism about the characteristics of a person called to live in God's presence. The psalmist begins with questions: "O Lord, who may abide in your tent? Who may dwell on your holy hill?"

The answer does not give specific names or classes, but sketches the character of the righteous person.

The qualities enumerated are both positive ("whoever walks blamelessly, and does what is right, and speaks the truth from their heart ...") and negative ("whoever does not slander with their tongue"). They are generic ("whoever does no evil to a friend") and specific ("whoever stands by their oath even to their hurt ... and does not take a bribe against the innocent").

Such instructions in the Old Testament, and others like them given by Jesus (for example, in the Sermon on the Mount), suggest prescriptions that must be fulfilled. To those who strive to please God, these instructions sometimes evoke frustration when they themselves seem unable to measure up to the ideal.

A different way of conceiving these formulas of right conduct is to see them as descriptions of what it is like to live under God's rule instead of relying on oneself.

James put it well when he observed that every example of goodness is already God's gift to his loved ones ("Every generous act of giving, with every perfect gift, is from above, coming down from the Father of lights").

Similarly, in the Book of Deuteronomy, Moses told the Israelites that the wonderful "statutes and ordinances" they were expected to observe showed God's special and unparalleled love for his people ("For what other great nation has a god so near to it as the Lord our God is whenever we call to him?").

What, then, is the disciple's role? Merely to receive the gift ("the implanted word that has the power to save your souls") and cooperate with its grace-filled dynamic so as to bear fruit pleasing to God ("be doers of the word, and not merely hearers"), not remain passive spectators.

As a prophet of social justice in the early Church, James listed some typical examples of "pure and undefiled" religious practice: "to care for orphans and widows in their distress, and to keep oneself unstained by the world".

The psalmist's reflection, therefore, asks people what they want to be like and whether they want and are trying to be like this. If one asked what God wanted, the traditional answer at the Jerusalem Temple was "sacrifice".

But we see in this psalm – which reflects the teaching of the prophets – that, more than sacrifice itself, God desired the proper inner dispositions that ought to have accompanied a sacrificial offering, namely a "broken heart" (cf. Psalm 51.16-17). The humble and contrite heart pleasing to God should hunger as well for what God wants: mercy, justice, righteousness, knowledge, goodness and love.

Today's rather complex gospel controversy engaged Jesus with the Pharisees and some of the scribes concerning what truly defiled – eating with unwashed hands or the sinful desires that sully the human heart. It is another example of the issue reflected on by the psalmist.

Jesus, in his teaching, moved the debate from a concern with externals to what comes from within a person. Jesus asked for behaviour that was congruent with God's will.

Jesus charged his enemies with making an external show of commitment to God's demands (lip service, really), while they passed over the break in their relationship with God ("their hearts are far from me").

In a radical departure, Jesus "declared all foods clean" (Mark 7.19) before going on to enumerate the sins that truly defile. The thirteen vices spell out what "evil intentions" lurk in the heart. This list has parallels elsewhere in the New Testament (e.g., Romans 1.29-31; Galatians 5.19-21; 1 Timothy 1.9-12; 2 Timothy 3.2-5) and in other Hellenistic Jewish writings.

Because he had broken with the categories inherited from Israel's community, Jesus could – without fear of "defilement" – touch a leper (Mark 1.41) and a corpse (in 5.41), eat with sinners (2.16-17), care for someone in the Decapolis territory of the unclean swine (5.2-19), and allow himself to be touched by a menstruating (= defiling) woman (5.27-28).

Thus, compassion typifies the person who possesses Jesus' new regard on what truly defiles.

Twenty-third Sunday in Ordinary Time

Jesus Heals: "Ephphatha: Be Opened!"

* Isaiah 35.4-7
* Psalm 146
* James 2.1-5
* Mark 7.31-37

The Exodus of God's people from bondage in Egypt became a model for thinking about salvation. The Second Isaiah (chapters 40–55) foretold the return of Jewish exiles from Babylon as a "new exodus".

This insight, in turn, inspired Isaiah's successors, writing in the fourth century B.C. (chapters 24–27 and 34–35), to apply the exodus motif to all God's saving deeds, now and in the future.

God's liberating activity touches the whole ecosystem as fresh vegetation replaces arid and depleted land ("the burning sand shall become a pool, and the thirsty ground springs of water"). God's saving power also embraces afflicted humans, healing every ill that comes upon people.

When God acts in favour of his beloved, the first evil driven out is fear ("Say to those who are of a fearful heart, 'Be strong, do not fear! Here is your God ... He will come and save you'").

Next the prophet addressed specific afflictions God would heal: "Then the eyes of the blind shall be opened, and the ears of the deaf unstopped; then the lame shall leap like a deer, and the tongue of the mute sing for joy". A new, coming era is envisioned; Jesus called it the reign of God, and he put it into effect during his ministry.

This text from Isaiah figured in Christ's reply to John the Baptist when he wondered about the things Jesus was doing and asked Jesus, "Are you the one who is to come, or are we to wait for another?" (cf. Matthew 11.2-6; Luke 7.18-23).

ARCHBISHOP TERRENCE PRENDERGAST

Isaiah's prediction may underlie Mark's understanding of Jesus' cure of "a man who was deaf and who had an impediment in his speech". One of the words used to describe the deaf-mute's problem means "could hardly speak" (in Greek, *mogilalos*) and is very rare. It appears only here in Mark in the New Testament and only in Isaiah 35.6 in the Greek version of the Old Testament.

In this way, and by means of his generalizing remark in the closing verse ("He has done everything well; he even makes the deaf to hear and the mute to speak"), Mark signalled to his readers the early Church's conviction that Jesus had inaugurated the end-time renewal of God's people that was foretold in Isaiah.

In healing the man, Jesus stuck his fingers into the man's ears, mimicking and thereby helping to open the ears to hear. The act of spitting, which symbolizes getting rid of something in the mouth that prevents speaking, helped to loosen the man's bound tongue. So did saliva from Jesus' healthy tongue.

The Aramaic word Jesus spoke ("*Ephphatha* ... Be opened!"), his look heavenwards and his groan all communicate the difficulty of the healing and the supernatural power Jesus needed to bring about the cure. A similar mix of a touching gesture and words may be seen in the difficult miracle of restoring Jairus' daughter to life (cf. Mark 5.40-42).

This healing of a person struggling to hear and speak plainly is paralleled with the healing in stages of the blind man of Bethsaida (Mark 8.22-26). Not only do these two miracles testify to Jesus' compassion, they also suggest what Jesus wished to do so that the Twelve and each disciple might see, speak and hear *spiritually* ("Do you have eyes, and fail to see? Do you have ears, and fail to hear?" [Mark 8.18]).

Through the whole of Mark's story, Jesus brought his followers to see, hear and speak about God's plan. He invited them to enter God's world view by accepting the cross in their lives, as he did. Possibly, the reason for the secrecy about Jesus' wonder-working power ("He took him aside in private, away from the crowd ... Then Jesus ordered them to tell no one") is to forestall people proclaiming his messiahship without telling about his suffering and death on the cross.

In every generation, as the psalmist says, "the Lord ... lifts up those who are bowed down". This includes not only Isaiah's visionary proclamation of the new exodus and Jesus' healing ministry, but also James' defence of the poor against those who would be partial to the rich ("Has not God chosen the poor in the world to be rich in faith and to be heirs of the kingdom that he has promised to those who love him?").

Twenty-fourth Sunday in Ordinary Time

The Centre of the Markan Gospel

* Isaiah 50.5-9
* Psalm 116
* James 2.14-18
* Mark 8.27-35

A few days before World Youth Day in the Great Jubilee Year 2000, the contingent I was accompanying had the joy of visiting the youth of a diocese south of Rome. Our encounter took place in the chapel of a Franciscan convent that dates back to the thirteenth century.

Tradition has it that Francis himself had lived in the area. He had dwelt there among thieves so as to share with them the joyful news of the reconciliation won for them by the death of Jesus.

At the close of our visit, there was an exchange of gifts. We offered our hosts some caps with our diocesan World Youth Day logo and copies of the archdiocesan jubilee CD. They presented us with scrolls containing the blessing of St. Francis, as well as the Franciscan *tau* cross, which many of the pilgrims wore from then on.

The *tau* is shaped like the capital "T" and – the Franciscans told us – was favoured by Francis because it was the last letter of the Hebrew alphabet and resembled the cross. In humility, Francis signed his letters with the *tau* as a sign of both his love of the cross of Christ and his desire to be considered last of all and least of all.

ARCHBISHOP TERRENCE PRENDERGAST

We do not know whether Francis was aware of it, but *tau* is also the first letter of the Hebrew word *teshuvah*. This word means "turning" and is the root meaning of the biblical and rabbinical concepts of "conversion".

Today's gospel reading is the centre and heart of Mark's Gospel. The confession at Caesarea Philippi occurs not only at the mid-point of the gospel, but at the place where the central issues of the gospel message come together.

Jesus' opening call to conversion (1.14-15) from now on takes the shape of a summons to each person who would be his follower to take up the cross and "follow me".

From the earliest verses of the gospel, people had wondered about Jesus and his activity ("What is this? A new teaching – with authority!" [1.27] ... "Who can forgive sins but God alone?" [2.7] ... "Who then is this, that even the wind and the sea obey him?" [4.41]). After long reflection, Peter – speaking on behalf of the Twelve – declared to Jesus, "You are the Christ".

As Jesus had earlier asked that people not speak of his healing miracles, he now asked that the apostles not reveal this truth of his status as Messiah ("He sternly ordered them not to tell anyone about him").

For Jesus will carry out his messianic mission in a totally unexpected way – by being handed over to crucifixion, being put to death and rising again "after three days".

As soon as Jesus began to explain how God intended him to fulfill his mission ("the Son of Man must ..."), Peter (again reflecting the thinking of his fellow apostles?) took Jesus aside "and began to rebuke him". In response, Jesus, "turning and looking at his disciples", rebuked Peter, indicating that Peter's way of looking at things had nothing to do with God's way of seeing things ("You are thinking not as God does, but as humans do").

The gospel material situated in Mark 8.27–10.52 consists of three passion predictions (8.31; 9.31; 10.33-34) followed by a series of vignettes about the behaviour of the apostles that shows they do not accept the implications of following a suffering messiah (8.32-

33; 9.32-34; 10.35-41), and additional new teaching by Jesus to help them live out their call to be his disciples (8.34-38; 9.35-37; 10.42-45).

The Twelve (and all disciples who hear the teaching of Jesus) are asked to have a change of mind and heart in regard to their behaviour. They follow a Messiah who was not a military hero but someone who suffered the fate of a criminal, exposed to death in the most brutal form of capital punishment known to the ancient world.

Disciples are invited to "lose their life for my sake and for the sake of the gospel" (8.35), to "be last of all and servant of all" (9.35) and "to be slave of all" in imitation of "the Son of Man [who] came not to be served but to serve, and to give his life as a ransom for many" (10.45).

We see, then, how well Francis of Assisi made his own the mind of his Master.

Twenty-fifth Sunday in Ordinary Time

"Those Conflicts and Disputes Among You"

* Wisdom 2.12, 17-20
* Psalm 54
* James 3.16–4.3
* Mark 9.30-37

For several weeks, the second reading is taken from the letter of James, "a servant of God and the Lord Jesus Christ [written] to the twelve tribes in the Dispersion" (1.1). The author – possibly James, "the brother (i.e., cousin) of the Lord" – has written an exhortation that challenges the faith of the early Christian community, probably from a base in the Palestine of the mid-first century.

At the outset, this letter seems to be nothing more than a collection of loosely connected aphorisms: "your anger does not produce

ARCHBISHOP TERRENCE PRENDERGAST

God's righteousness" (1.20); "Do you not know that friendship with the world is enmity with God?" (4.4); "Draw near to God, and he will draw near to you" (4.8).

Further study, however, reveals a summary opening chapter (1.1-27) – an overture, as it were – that is followed by a closely structured (if somewhat circular) argument. Some of the conflicts Christians need to come to terms with, James argues, include the incompatibility of faith with discrimination (2.1-11), the inadequacy of faith without deeds (2.14-26), and the misuse of one's tongue and speech (3.1-12).

James contrasts friendship with the world and friendship with God, from which today's second reading is drawn (3.13–4.10), righteously denounces offenses involving the misuse of property (4.13–5.6), proposes a right outlook towards the end (5.7-11), and suggests a proper use of speech within the community of believers (5.13-18). This last text includes the beautiful passage on the anointing of the sick by the elders of the church that is so dear to the Catholic community.

In his *Anchor Bible Commentary* on James, Luke Timothy Johnson asserts that "no other text of the ancient world offers as rich a set of reflections on the grounds for violence and peace in the world as does James" (New York: Doubleday, 1995, p. 164).

As well, almost alone among the New Testament writings, James provides a solid basis for social ethics. For James prophetically condemns the oppression of the poor by the exploitative rich (5.1-6). Equally strongly, he criticizes any discrimination between human beings on the basis of appearance (2.1-7). James portrays the power and perils of the gift of human speech (3.1-12) and locates the roots of social conflict, war and murder in the skewed logic of envy (3.13–4.10).

Today's second reading consists in James' indictment of human envy; its conclusion – beyond the lectionary selection – proposes the humbling of oneself before God as the solution: "Humble yourselves before the Lord, and he will exalt you" (4.10).

The movement upward in self-assertion, which envy manifests, must be countered, James says, with a posture of meekness that shows oneself ready and able to receive gifts from God above. This is the antidote to human grasping for self-aggrandizement and the false notion that one possesses status with God and others on the basis of possessions or a position of authority or power.

"Those conflicts and disputes among you ... come from your cravings that are at war within you". Not having something leads one to "commit murder" (we do not know whether James means this literally or figuratively), and coveting leads you to "engage in disputes and conflicts".

In today's gospel, Jesus noticed that the disciples were arguing. When he inquired about the topic of their dispute, they were silent, sensing perhaps that an argument about status among themselves was inappropriate.

Jesus taught a way to greatness that passed by way of lowliness and service. Its model was the child. Though our social conventions idealize childhood, the child was a nonentity in the world of Jesus, belonging with the women and not with the Teacher or his students. It was inconceivable in the first-century Mediterranean world to suggest that receiving a child would have meaning for the male disciples. Yet, the child becomes a stand-in for Jesus – and for God, who sent him!

Asking who would be first among them was to ask who would stand in the place of Jesus. Jesus' answer was that his representative must be willing to be like a child ("last of all") and a slave ("servant of all").

Jesus drew his disciples into the paradoxical mystery of a suffering that redeems. These were the first lessons in the drama of the cross, the trial of an innocent individual already anticipated by the testing of the righteous in the Book of Wisdom.

These "passion predictions" are, in each case, followed by some gesture by the disciples that illustrates their incomprehension of – or resistance to – Jesus' teaching (8.32-33; 9.33-34; 10.35-41). Each time, Jesus patiently explored with the disciples the implications of following a despised and rejected messiah (8.34–9.1; 9.35-37; 10.42-45).

Twenty-sixth Sunday in Ordinary Time

Jesus' Tolerance, Fire and Judgment

* Numbers 11.25-29
* Psalm 19
* James 5.1-6
* Mark 9.38-43, 45, 47-48

Today's gospel is an amalgam of sayings of Jesus on a variety of topics. The different sayings have become associated by means of catchwords: "name" (Mark 9.38, 39, 41), "cause to stumble" (42, 43, 45, 47), "hell" (43, 45, 47), "fire" (43, 45, 47, 48, 49) and "salt" (49, 50), possibly mnemonic devices to help people remember Jesus' sayings while they were being handed on in oral form.

Verses 44 and 46 do not appear in modern versions of the Bible. Identical with verse 48 ("where their worm never dies, and the fire is never quenched"), they are not found in the best ancient manuscripts.

The episode leading into these sayings depicts Jesus urging his disciples to a tolerant spirit when they wished to curb an exorcist who is found casting out demons in Jesus' name. It is ironic that several verses earlier, these same disciples had been unable to perform an exorcism (Mark 9.14-29).

As spokesman for the Twelve, John said that they had forbidden the exorcist "because he was not following us". Jesus cautioned them, saying they should not put constraints on the outsider exorcist ("Do not stop him"). For, Jesus argued, such a person could not simultaneously use Jesus' name to perform an exorcism and immediately ("soon afterward") slander him.

Now, to be effective as an exorcist, the individual had to have had enough regard for the name that he would not slander it. Otherwise, if he thought little of Jesus' name, it would prove ineffective in the exorcism being attempted. Jesus concluded his admonition to the disciples with a most gracious statement in regard to others: "whoever is not against us is for us".

In the reading from Numbers, we see Moses manifesting a similar generosity of spirit when Joshua wanted to put a stop to two unauthorized individuals (Eldad and Medad) who were given the gift of prophecy.

Earlier, Moses had complained to God about the burdens of leading the chosen people. In response, God took some of the spirit of Moses and gave it to seventy elders who were chosen to assist Moses with the leadership tasks.

In response to the gift of the spirit that had been in Moses, these elders prophesied. But in contrast with Moses' unique and ongoing gift of prophecy, these elders received the prophetic gift for this one occasion ("When the spirit rested on them, they prophesied. But they did not do so again").

Somehow when the spirit of Moses was being shared with the seventy elders, some spilled over onto two people who were in their tents and not with the seventy at the tabernacle. Joshua asked Moses to stop such a runaway expression of God's spirit by exercising his authority over them. In response, Moses assured Joshua that he welcomed such a manifestation of God's insight among the people, as he had welcomed it among the seventy leaders ("Would that all the Lord's people were Prophets, and that the Lord would put his spirit on them!")

Though Jesus corrected the narrow viewpoint of John and the other disciples, he still chose to associate himself with them ("whoever gives you a cup of water to drink because you bear the name of Christ will by no means lose the reward"). This approach simply continues Jesus' process of patiently leading the disciples to understand what it means to follow him.

In the subsequent sayings, Jesus emphasized the need to maintain one's status as a disciple by avoiding sins that would undermine an authentic following of him. The stark and startling sayings that it is better to "enter [eternal] life" maimed or lame or with one eye than being whole "and to go to hell" describe the stakes in following Jesus.

The English word "hell" translates *Gehenna*, the garbage dump of Jerusalem in the Hinnon Valley where a fire burned continuously and maggots consumed the refuse. Gehenna/hell became a figure for the end-time and unending torment of sinners who choose the path of unrighteousness rather than virtue.

James used similar imagery to excoriate wealthy unbelievers who perpetrated injustice against poor Christians. The material goods in which they had put their trust would soon fail them ("Your riches have rotted, and your clothes are moth-eaten. Your gold and silver have rusted, and their rust will be evidence against you, and it will eat your flesh like fire").

Twenty-seventh Sunday in Ordinary Time

The Permanence of Marriage

* Genesis 2.7ab, 8b, 18-24
* Psalm 128
* Hebrews 2.9-11
* Mark 10.2-16

Jesus' teaching on divorce is widely attested in the New Testament (cf. Matthew 5.32; 19.6, 9; Mark 10.9; Luke 16.18; 1 Corinthians 7.11). Yet, apart from Matthew 19.6b and Mark 10.9, none of these sayings agrees in every detail with the others. The issues involved are complex; this fact underlines the different understandings of marriage and divorce in various Christian churches.

Roman Catholic teaching sees in marriage "a covenant by which a man and a woman establish between themselves a partnership of their whole life and which of its own very nature is ordered to the well-being of the spouses and to the procreation and upbringing of children" (Canon 1055).

Fundamental to a person's being able to enter into such a marital covenant is their freedom to give consent to a lifelong commitment to the other. If their free consent is missing or seriously flawed, there is no marriage. In such cases, marriage tribunals may issue a declaration of nullity (an annulment). An annulment does not make a marriage invalid; it simply declares that it always was invalid, despite appearances to the contrary.

The introduction to today's gospel passage omits the setting given by Mark's narrative: namely, that Jesus left Capernaum and went to the region of Judea and beyond the Jordan, where crowds gathered and Jesus taught them (10.1).

This region beyond the Jordan, Perea, is likely the place where John the Baptist had been imprisoned in the fortress of Machareus. There he had been beheaded, in part because of his objections to Herod Antipas' behaviour in divorcing his wife in order to marry his brother's former wife (Mark 6.17-19).

John the Baptist's commitment to the sanctity of marriage cost him his life. And it is possible that the political implications of Jesus' giving similar teaching in regard to marriage underlies the comment that the Pharisees asked their question on divorce ("Is it lawful for a man to divorce his wife?") "to test Jesus".

Jesus used his exchange with the Pharisees to bring out the deeper sense of the Scriptures. He admitted that in Deuteronomy 24.1, Moses commanded that a "certificate of dismissal" be given to the divorced wife, but said it was because of "your hardness of heart".

Moses had tried to limit the negative effects of divorce by showing mercy towards the divorced wife. Jesus, however, preached the coming kingdom of God, which does not belong to the hard-hearted and faithless people with whom he contended in his ministry.

Jesus pointed to God's plan in creating man and woman, citing two texts from Genesis: 1.27 ("from the beginning of creation 'God made them male and female'") and 2.24 ("For this reason a man shall leave his father and mother and be joined to his wife, and the two shall become one flesh").

Jesus grounded his teaching on the order of creation, God's intention in creating human beings. In marriage, man and woman are "no longer two, but one flesh". Jesus' concluding remark, "what God has joined together, let no one separate", is the conclusion to the debate engaged with his contemporaries. Jesus taught that God had created man and woman so that they might be joined together in the unity of one flesh in marriage.

When the disciples asked Jesus in the house to spell out the implications of his teaching, he asserted that remarriage after divorce constitutes adultery. In effect, Jesus said that the prohibition of adultery by the sixth commandment takes precedence over the toleration in Deuteronomy 24.1 of divorce.

Jewish law allowed only a husband to divorce his wife, whereas Greco-Roman law allowed either party to divorce the other. The closing verse ("if she divorces her husband and marries another, she commits adultery") shows the universal applicability of Jesus' teaching.

To accept the teaching of Jesus on marriage and divorce – and other areas of life – requires a conversion of heart, a rebirth. Jesus called for this conversion in the reproach he gave his disciples for hindering little children from coming to him ("whoever does not receive the kingdom of God as a little child will never enter it").

Jesus identified with those who were dependent, who were held to be of no account. In the words of the letter to the Hebrews, "[Jesus] is not ashamed to call them brothers and sisters".

Twenty-eighth Sunday in Ordinary Time

The Danger and Challenge of Riches

* Wisdom 7.7-11
* Psalm 90
* Hebrews 4.12-13
* Mark 10.17-30

The Letter to the Hebrews is an extended exhortation to Christians who had been growing weary with the cost of discipleship towards the end of the first century. The author blended esoteric interpretation of the scriptures with truly beautiful reflections on God's word and on the humanity of Christ. Indeed, Jesus is God's word made visible, manifesting God's compassion and encouragement.

The description of God's word as "living and active, sharper than any two-edged sword ... able to judge the thoughts and intentions of the heart" came true in the meeting Jesus had with the rich man in today's gospel. Jesus' dialogue uncovered the attachment of that clean-living man ("I have kept all these [commandments] since my youth") to his "many possessions".

The wealthy man had everything except that missing something ("what must I do to inherit eternal life?") that gnawed at his conscience. His riches let him have all he could ever have wanted, except freedom to heed Jesus' command to "go, sell what you own, and give the money to the poor, and you will have treasure in heaven; then come, follow me".

Two millennia after this episode, the teaching of Jesus about riches still has the power to unsettle his disciples, as it did the man Jesus loved and watched go away "grieving". Initially, someone reading the story today might wonder whether Jesus meant his challenge only for particular individuals, or might ask whether Jesus' challenge regarding riches touches everyone, to a degree.

We might observe that Mother Teresa was already vowed to religious poverty when she heard Jesus call her to devote herself to the "poorest of the poor". Jesus' comments after the rich man left him suggest that his comments have a wide, if not universal, applicability.

We learn that the disciples were perplexed at the trenchant words of their Lord: "How hard it will be for those who have wealth to enter the kingdom of God! ... It is easier for a camel to go through the eye of a needle than for someone who is rich to enter the kingdom of God".

Frustrated, the disciples asked Jesus, "Then who can be saved?" For they shared the view of their contemporaries that riches were a sign of God's blessing and of the rich person's good standing with God. Jesus had another view of matters dealing with money and the effects it could have on people.

ARCHBISHOP TERRENCE PRENDERGAST

A study of millionaire philanthropists some time ago revealed that they reckoned power and influence – the ability to get things done – as the most significant advantage of wealth. Yet in the key section of his teaching – about the impact of taking up the cross on the lives of his disciples (Mark 8.31–10.52) – Jesus constantly undermined his disciples' attraction to power by demanding that they lower their expectations of power, even becoming powerless like children (9.35-37; 10.14-16).

In this case, surrendering one's riches implies letting go of the power and status associated with them to embrace the lowliness of Jesus and the poor. When the issue is salvation, humans are helpless ("for humans it is impossible").

Salvation, entering the kingdom, inheriting eternal life – all these ways of describing the ultimate issue – are God's unmerited gift. "For God all things are possible", even the salvation of a wealthy person!

To the person who surrendered ties to wealth in its various guises (money, power, knowledge, influence), Jesus paradoxically offered a hundred-fold return ("but with persecutions") in this world. Jesus pledged to disciples who leave all, for his sake and the gospel's, that "now in this age" they would share with other church members other possessions and family members instead of those they had surrendered. Best of all, Jesus promised "in the age to come, eternal life".

Jesus called for discernment and wisdom about what was truly important in life. In the Book of Wisdom, Solomon was depicted as having prayed God for "understanding" and the "spirit of wisdom", preferring these to trappings of power ("sceptres and thrones"). Because he reckoned wisdom greater than "any priceless gem" and thought "gold [was] but a little sand in her sight", he, too, experienced Jesus' paradoxical viewpoint ("all good things came to me along with [wisdom])".

Servant Leaders of Jesus the High Priest

* Isaiah 53.10-11
* Psalm 33
* Hebrews 4.14-16
* Mark 10.35-45

A singular contribution of the Letter to the Hebrews to Christian understanding of Jesus lies in its designation of him as the High Priest of the New Covenant. Earlier, this brilliant first-century interpreter stated this thesis: "[Jesus] had to become like his brothers and sisters in every respect, so that he might be a merciful and faithful high priest in the service of God, to make a sacrifice of atonement for the sins of the people" (2.17).

The implication of this high priestly motif is striking: "because Jesus himself was tested by what he suffered, he is able to help those who are being tested". Christians struggling to be faithful to their calling may take comfort that their Lord understands them because he, too, experienced testing. "We do not have a high priest who is unable to sympathize with our weaknesses, but we have one who in every respect has been tested as we are, yet without sin".

Jesus' empathy with his disciples leads him to continue now, in heaven, his intercession for them at God's right hand. In stressing Christ's sympathy for humanity, our Christian homilist underlined his capacity to help those who are helpless.

The emphatic statement that Jesus was tempted "in every respect, as we are" implies he was susceptible to all the temptations associated with the frailty of the human condition. In the gospel tradition, this truth is communicated by the stories of Jesus' temptations in the wilderness after his baptism (cf. Matthew 4.1-13) as well as by his "agony" in the Garden of Gethsemane at the beginning of the passion (cf. Mark 14.32-42).

The conclusion is that Christians should not hold back from manifesting to the Lord Jesus their need of help. "Let us therefore approach the throne of grace with boldness, so that we may receive mercy and find grace to help in time of need".

When readers consider the self-serving expectations of James and John ("Grant us to sit, one at your right hand and one at your left, in your glory"), it is easy to judge them harshly. Yet Jesus did not do so. Knowing how idealism and ambition can easily get mixed together in a person's psyche, Christ explored with them their differing outlooks, in order to set them free from their narrow self-interest towards his generous self-offering.

Jesus did not rebuke James and John. When they said they were able to drink his cup and be baptized with his baptism, he accepted their assertion but set their motives right. They thought the cup and the baptism were means to glory, but he taught them to see these as means to fellowship with him and as the only way to follow him through death to resurrection life. Accepting the disciples as they were, Jesus led them onto the path he would walk.

The other ten "began to be angry with James and John", but we should scarcely expect that it was because they had a different disposition. Rather, we must imagine it was because they were jealous that the sons of Zebedee had got their bid in ahead of the others.

Jesus patiently explained that in the kingdom of God ("among you"), things had to be different than in the world of power relationships ("among the Gentiles those whom they recognize as their rulers lord it over them"). Jesus' way is summarized in a couple of maxims: "Whoever wishes to become great among you must be your servant, and whoever wishes to be first among you must be slave of all".

Believing disciples need to make their own the disposition of Christ, who filled the role of the mysterious suffering servant of God that Isaiah spoke of ("[he] shall make many righteous, and he shall bear their iniquities").

Jesus let his followers learn that true discipleship manifests itself in a costly pouring out of one's life for another, whether it be for an aging parent, a difficult spouse, a special child or some neighbour whose need becomes known.

"For the Son of Man came not to be served but to serve, and to give his life as a ransom for many". Only Jesus redeems, but others are invited to pour out their lives to benefit others as he did.

Thirtieth Sunday in Ordinary Time

To See and Follow Jesus

* Jeremiah 31.7-9
* Psalm 126
* Hebrews 5.1-6
* Mark 10.46-52

The message of the prophets constantly linked references to what God had done for Israel in the past with what God was about to do in the future. Thus, the Exodus became a model for the liberation God would effect for those sent into exile from Samaria, the northern kingdom that fell in 721 B.C., and from Jerusalem, which suffered conquest in 587.

As the prophet Jeremiah proclaimed God's coming salvation, he invited the people to declare, in anticipation, God's praises ("Sing aloud with gladness … and say 'Save, O Lord, your people, the remnant of Israel'").

Hope grew that what God had begun to do with the tiniest remnant – those who were weak and least able to fend for themselves – God would extend to all who heard the Good News of salvation ("I am going to … gather them from the farthest parts of the earth, … those who are blind and those who are lame, those with child and those in labour, together; a great company, they shall return here").

The contrast between eyes weeping as they see the desolation being inflicted and the consolation of return is captured well by the responsorial psalm ("may those who sow in tears reap with shouts of joy").

ARCHBISHOP TERRENCE PRENDERGAST

Liberation, which had seemed inconceivable, has come true ("When the Lord restored the fortunes of Zion, we were like those who dream. Then our mouth was filled with laughter, and our tongue with shouts of joy").

The healing of blind Bartimaeus is the last miracle of Jesus narrated in Mark's Gospel. This cure constitutes the conclusion to the discipleship section (8.31–10.52) and prepares for the ministry that Jesus will carry on in Jerusalem.

Jesus' words to Bartimaeus ("What do you want me to do for you?") are identical with his query to James and John in last Sunday's reading. Their misguided request for positions of power on that occasion is corrected by the enlightened hope of a blind man that he might see again.

As well, the story's conclusion ("the man regained his sight and followed Jesus on the way") makes the behaviour of Bartimaeus a model for disciples of Jesus. The text invites the reader or hearer to come to Jesus and see; seeing aright implies following Jesus.

The difficulties Bartimaeus faced in regaining his sight make him an ideal case study of faith. At the gates of the city of Jericho where the blind and other beggars sought alms, the son of Timaeus heard that Jesus of Nazareth was passing by. Bartimaeus called out to him in words that have become known as "the Jesus Prayer" ("Jesus, Son of David, have mercy on me!").

In his book *Learning to Pray*, the Orthodox Metropolitan Anthony Bloom says that Bartimaeus is an example for all Christians who would live a life of prayer. Many find themselves facing difficulties – external and internal – to the act of praying. The difficulties of Bartimaeus, which he overcame, issued from the crowds who wanted to stifle his appeal to Jesus ("Many sternly ordered him to be quiet, but he cried out even more loudly").

Once the obstacles in prayer are faced, they seem minor. When Jesus stopped and sought Bartimaeus out, even the crowds changed their tune ("Take heart; get up, he is calling you"). Encouraged by Jesus' interest, Bartimaeus was able to give voice to his deepest longing: "My teacher, let me see again".

Jesus, stressing the faith that underlay this petition, reassured Bartimaeus, "Go; your faith has made you well". As the ideal pray-er, Bartimaeus expressed the desire of his heart persistently, simply and honestly. "Immediately the man regained his sight".

The paralleling of the roles of the Levitical priest and the priest-hood of Jesus extends a few verses beyond today's second reading (Hebrews 5.1-10). At the centre of this description we find stress placed on every priest's humility and solidarity with people ("He is able to deal gently with the ignorant and wayward, since he is himself subject to weakness").

The Old Testament priest did not presume his office ("one does not presume to take this honour, but takes it only when called by God"). Neither did Jesus, who belongs to the order of Melchizedek and whose task was to create an order of salvation that is valid forever.

Thirty-first Sunday in Ordinary Time

Love More Important Than All Sacrifices

* Deuteronomy 6.2-6
* Psalm 18
* Hebrews 7.23-28
* Mark 12.28-34

Some years ago, the Plenary Assembly of the Canadian Conference of Catholic Bishops released a document inviting Catholics to grow in appreciation of the Church's relationship with the Jewish people.

Titled *Jubilee*, the six-page pamphlet speaks of "renewing our common bonds with the Jewish community". Nowhere is this bond clearer than in the Sunday liturgy, where the first reading and the psalm are regularly drawn from the Old Testament.

ARCHBISHOP TERRENCE PRENDERGAST

Today's first reading includes the beginning of a text known by the Jewish people as the *Shema* ("Hear, O Israel") [Deuteronomy 6.4-9]. This declaration of faith is so important that observant Jews recite it every morning, and it is found embedded in a small cylinder known as the mezuzah posted at the entry to their homes ("write [these words] on the doorposts of your house and on your gates" [6.9]).

This formula binds every true Israelite to hear and obey the truth that the Lord is one God, the only deity to be worshipped by God's chosen people. It is not an explicit confession of *monotheism* (the belief that there is only one God), though for Israel all energy is to be directed to serving the Lord.

The text allows for *henotheism* – belief that there are other gods, among whom the Lord was to be worshipped by Israel – because, when this text was composed, people generally held that each nation had its own proper deity.

As Israel's faith deepened over the centuries, mounting evidence from the Old Testament shows that Israel recognized what was implied by the *Shema*: namely, that there was only one God.

This one God, who had been revealed to Moses and who had intervened in history to save the Hebrews from bondage in Egypt, was gradually understood to be the only God, Creator of heaven and earth and Redeemer of all men and women under heaven, beginning with Israel.

In gratitude for this privileged awareness given to the chosen people, the Lord had to be loved: not conditionally and half-heartedly, but unconditionally and without reserve ("You shall love the Lord your God with all your heart, and with all your soul, and with all your might").

It may seem odd that love is commanded, but what is envisaged here is deep loyalty and affection for God's rescue of his people from slavery and the coming gift of the Promised Land (the Book of Deuteronomy represents the last testament of Moses to Israel as the people prepare to enter a land flowing with milk and honey): "Keep these words that I am commanding you today in your heart".

As *Jubilee* points out, "Jesus was born of the Jewish people, and was rooted in the tradition of Moses and the prophets. Although his teaching had a profoundly new character, in many instances Christ took his stand on the teachings of the Hebrew Scriptures and often employed the methods of the rabbis of his time".

When asked about the first of all the commandments, Jesus made his own the *Shema*, the confession that the Lord God is one, then summarized the Law as the double commandment to love God totally and, citing Leviticus 19.18, to love one's neighbour as oneself.

The scribe repeated Jesus' answer, drawing the right conclusion that this two-fold love is "much more important than all whole burnt offerings and sacrifices". In biblical thought, sacrifices were efficacious when they were accompanied by a contrite heart that overflows into love of God and love of neighbour.

Though in Mark's Gospel the scribes are almost universally depicted in a negative light, in this instance the scribe's insight merited Jesus' approval ("You are not far from the kingdom of God"). If we were to ask what further step, in the evangelist's perspective, the scribe must take to inherit or enter the kingdom, it seems the Markan Jesus' answer would involve some such reply as "go now and put into practice the conclusion you have correctly drawn".

The Letter to the Hebrews concludes that the priesthood of Jesus differed from biblical antecedents in several ways, chiefly in that he offered his life on the cross "once for all".

Now, Jesus' priesthood continues in heaven, where "he always lives to make intercession" and "to save those who approach God through him".

Thirty-second Sunday in Ordinary Time

"She Has Put in Everything ..."

* 1 Kings 17.10-16
* Psalm 146
* Hebrews 9.24-28
* Mark 12.38-44

In our diocese of Ottawa, a small committee works with great determination to propose the concept of stewardship. Inspired by a pastoral letter, "Stewardship – A Disciple's Response", written by the United States Bishops Conference, committee members invite their fellow Catholics to consider a foundational truth: that all they have received has been entrusted to them by God to use wisely.

Gratitude for the gifts one has received from God will, in this view, lead the disciple of Jesus to want to share with the parish community a generous portion of his or her time, talent and treasure.

The American bishops were aware that stewardship had not been part of Catholic tradition, and that cynics might argue it was simply a new means of raising money for church purposes. Indeed, our Church has tended to operate much more on the principle that people will give what is needed as it is needed.

The bishops knew that they had to redirect the focus away from here-and-now material needs towards a spiritual disposition based on the conversion of each disciple's outlook.

A question often asked by religious leaders in the past was "What does the Church need to carry out the mission?" However, the really important question to put to a disciple could better be formulated as "What has God given me that I need to steward according to God's will?"

For disciples of Jesus to be stewards, they must first come to the realization that what they have – time, talent and treasure (money) – belongs to God, and that they are simply caretakers of these precious gifts.

To be a steward and to share one's time and talent with one's faith community involves entering into the spirit of sacrificial giving. Then the generous sharing of one's treasure follows naturally; it, too, cannot help but be sacrificial. The widow in today's gospel passage reveals that far more important than the amount given is the spirit of surrender to God with which one gives.

In Jerusalem, during his last days, Jesus excoriated the scribes for loving the kind of attention accorded religious leaders: recognition in public, the best seats in the sacred assembly and "places of honour at banquets". Instead of humility, such attention can induce pride and even preying on the needy to get the money required to keep up one's image ("They devour widows' houses and for the sake of appearance say long prayers").

Instead, Jesus directed his focus onto the inner disposition of humble giving by a widow, in contrast with outer displays of munificence by the wealthy. Jesus surprised his hearers with the remark that "this poor widow has put in more than all those who are contributing to the treasury. For all of them have contributed out of their abundance; but she out of her poverty has put in everything she had, all she had to live on".

In proportion to their resources, the large sums contributed by the rich involved no real sacrifice on their part. So they cannot compare with the widow's tiny gift, which was a sacrifice of all she had to live on. Mark tells us that the two copper pieces she put in were two *lepta*, the smallest coins in circulation, and – Mark translated for his readers – made up a Roman quadrans ("which are worth a penny"). This came to 1/64 of a denarius, the daily wage of a labourer.

The widow of Zarephath showed a similar self-sacrificing disposition, offering to the prophet Elijah a portion of the little she had to keep herself alive. Her reward was a miracle that fed her, her son and the prophet "for many days".

Jesus implied that discipleship involves absolute surrender to God's will and purpose, a disposition to which he would recommit himself in his passion. Jesus' self-sacrifice, mirrored in the widow's offering, is highlighted by the author of Hebrews.

Formerly the high priest entered the Holy of Holies each year with blood belonging to animals ("with blood that is not his own"), whereas Christ offered his own life in atonement for the sins of the world. "[Christ] has appeared once for all at the end of the age to remove sin by the sacrifice of himself".

Thirty-third Sunday in Ordinary Time

"About That Day or Hour No One Knows"

* Daniel 12.1-3
* Psalm 16
* Hebrews 10.11-14, 18
* Mark 13.24-32

The author of the Letter to the Hebrews strove in 10.1-18 to show how Jesus acted as "the source of eternal salvation for all who obey him" (5.9b). Earlier he had presented the "objective" results of Christ' self-offering. Through his entrance into the heavenly sanctuary, Jesus had fulfilled God's eternal plan of redemption (9.11-28).

Now, our evangelist focuses on the "subjective" dimension of salvation: the effects of Christ's sacrifice upon the community of believers who enjoy the blessings flowing from Jesus' saving deed on the cross.

In the polemical teaching of Hebrews, the Levitical priests were contrasted with Christ. Though they stood day after day offering sacrifices, their priesthood was unable to remove sins ("offering again and again the same sacrifices that can never take away sins").

By contrast, once Jesus' unique and totally adequate sacrifice had taken place, "he sat down at the right hand of God". Jesus is shown seated because his sacrifice requires no repetition. Rather, his session in God's presence attests that the benefits of his sacrifice endure forever.

Christ Jesus now waits in heaven "until his enemies would be made a footstool for his feet". This citation of Psalm 110.1 (frequently used to refer to Christ's resurrection) argues that Jesus' status is firmly established. There will be no need of a new high priest or sacrifice. It also points to that moment – hidden in God's purposes – when every power that resists God's gracious design and redemptive purpose will be defeated and become subject to God's will.

That end-time moment, which preoccupied the prophet Daniel (first reading), is the subject of Jesus' apocalyptic teaching in today's gospel. The words read or heard today are a call to turn from historical circumstances and futuristic signs to the culmination of all things with the coming of Christ ("Then they will see 'the Son of Man coming in clouds' with great power and glory").

In citing Daniel 7.13, which described the son of man's ascent to the divine throne, Jesus reoriented it, giving it significance also for those on earth. Jesus' coming in clouds would precede his sending angels to gather in the elect – "from the four winds, from the ends of the earth to the ends of heaven" – so that no one would be left out.

These are consoling words for Christians, as were Jesus' earlier words that those enduring to the end would be saved (Mark 13.13) and that "for the sake of the elect" God would shorten the end-time travails (13.20).

The awesome description of the turmoil in the astronomical bodies ("the sun will be darkened, and the moon will not give its light, and the stars will be falling from heaven, and the powers in the heavens will be shaken") indicates a cessation of the functions God had given these in creation (Genesis 1.14-19).

Jesus linked his description of the end to something visible every year in Palestine: the fig tree's leaves signal the coming of summer. One must be observant to make this connection; just so, one needs to be ever vigilant for the coming of the end.

Jesus gave another reason for watchfulness: "about that hour or day no one knows, neither the Angels in heaven, nor the Son, but only the Father".

From time to time, we may expect an outpouring of prophecies that the end times are arriving, sent through some visionary or privileged personality. Still, "about that hour or day no one knows," not even "the Son".

The enduring validity of Jesus' word on this subject ("Heaven and earth will pass away, but my words will not pass away") saves Christian disciples worry and anxiety.

But not from the challenge of being vigilant: believers are to watch for Christ's coming, for them personally in death or to usher in the end of the world.

Daniel contains the most developed Old Testament teaching about the resurrection. In the end days ("a time of anguish, such as has never occurred since nations first came into existence"), the Archangel Michael will come to comfort God's people.

After their resurrection, the faithful ones will share in God's glory. "Those who are wise shall shine like the brightness of the sky, and those who lead many to righteousness, like the stars forever and ever".

Thirty-fourth Sunday in Ordinary Time:
Christ the King

A Kingdom of Priests for God

* Daniel 7.13-14
* Psalm 93
* Revelation 1.5-8
* John 18.33-37

In his ministry, Jesus proclaimed the kingdom of God. In parables, he described its mysterious presence in the world and invited his hearers to heed its demands. Christ's exorcisms and miracles gave evidence that, though the kingdom had a future dimension, it had drawn near by restoring people to health and life. When Jesus instructed his disciples about prayer, he taught them to pray to God "thy kingdom come".

The notion of God as a king ruling his people began with the Judges and Samuel. Some interpreted Israel's decision to have a king like the nations around them as being a rejection of God's kingly reign over them. Others saw that God ruled his people through the king.

The experience of wicked kings and the dissolution of the monarchy stirred up in prophets and sages the hope that God would again hold sway over all his chosen ones. They would then be a holy nation, sharing in God's rule as kings and priests. Whether God's rule then would be direct or through a designated individual remained a matter of debate.

Besides introducing the notion of a double resurrection (last Sunday's readings), the Book of Daniel also had a powerful impact on New Testament notions of the kingdom of God. In Daniel's vision he spoke of one "like a son of man" on whom the "Ancient of Days" ("Ancient One") would confer "dominion and glory and kingship". This dominion would be "everlasting" and worldwide, for "all peoples, nations and languages should serve him": a kingship never to be destroyed.

In Ezekiel, the term "son of man" (lowercase letters) had a pedestrian sense, much like referring to someone as a "human being." When God addressed Ezekiel as "son of man," the *New Revised Standard Version* translates this as "mortal."

In Daniel, the title "Son of man" (capitalized) clearly refers to a heavenly figure who shares human characteristics. The *New Revised Standard Version* uses "human being" here, but this wording may miss some idea of this figure's exalted status.

In the gospels, the term "Son of Man" is found only on the lips of Jesus. Scholars have had enormous difficulty in sorting out how Jesus meant this self-designation. Are we to understand references to himself as the Son of Man (for example in Mark 2.28, "the Son of Man is Lord of the Sabbath") in a lowercase sense (that is, meaning simply "I")? Or are they to be understood in an exalted or capital letters sense (as in Mark 13.26: "they will see 'the Son of man coming in clouds'")?

Some think Jesus used the ambiguity of the title to both conceal and reveal his identity as the royal Son who fulfilled Old Testament prophecies and hopes.

Thus, Jesus' royal dignity could be publicly manifest only during the passion, when no one would misunderstand his kingship as being of this world or being one of power. Jesus declared his kingly role only during his trial. In the Synoptic Gospels, his declaration is made before the Sanhedrin (cf. Mark 14.62); in John it is made to Pilate (John 19.8-11). There Jesus, broken and abased in human weakness, sat in judgment on the one who thought he had power over Jesus. For in his dialogue with Pilate, Jesus always seems to have the upper hand.

Jesus declared that the tokens of his kingship were not power or status but truth and a right relationship with God. Jesus declared that anyone open to the truth "listens to my voice". For his intent was his Father's – to draw all the scattered children of God into the one fold he shepherded. The true king ruled not as Herod or Pilate, but as a shepherd deals with wounded sheep in tenderness and compassion.

In the text from Revelation, John, the seer of Patmos, reflected on what Christ Jesus has accomplished by his love for sinners and "by his blood" shed for the life of the world. John said that Christ had set Christians free and "made us to be a kingdom", subjects of his.

Not only that, "the firstborn of the dead" had given all the members of his kingdom a share in his priestly ministry, "serving his God and Father".